Stop Thinking, Start Living, & Begin Celebrating Every Moment

Stop Thinking, Start Living, & Begin Celebrating Every Moment

The Renaissance M. A. N.

Renaissance Publishing

For further information, please contact:
Startliving@mac.com
Liveandcelebrate.com

Book designed by:
Arbor Books, Inc.
19 Spear Road, Suite 301
Ramsey, NJ 07446
www.arborbooks.com

Printed in the United States of America

Stop Thinking, Start Living, and Begin Celebrating Every Moment
The Renaissance M.A.N., Michael A. Nardi

1. Title 2. Author 3. Self-Help/Spiritual

Library of Congress Control Number: 2007929919

ISBN-10: 0-9797017-0-8
ISBN-13: 978-0-9797017-0-2

*I dedicate this book to Billy for teaching me to dream
and Domenico for starting my path.*

*In loving memory of Momma J (1952-2007),
who taught me to celebrate every moment of my life.*

Table of Contents

Acknowledgements

I want to thank my family and friends for making this possible: Thanks for always listening to my dreams no matter how crazy they sounded. I want to thank my mother for giving me the wings to fly and for always encouraging to use them. She has been the greatest inspiration in my life; being named after her has been a blessing of unparalleled consequence. She has taught me how to improve the quality of the world around me. I want to thank my father for always teaching me to dream and for our new friendship. Thank you, Momma J and my new dad, for always believing in Ashley and I. Bob, thanks for your presence and for showing me how to be content in life. Thank you, Billy, for teaching me to write. Thanks, Colleen, for always pushing me to new possibilities. Nicky, I thank you for the energy you put into your work; Mike, for your modeling; Aimee, for your stories; Alison, for your wisdom; and Anna, for your love you have brought into the family.

After sitting in the hospital and watching my mother-in-law in pain, I realized it was time for me to begin this process. The next day when she was feeling better, we were driving and having a very nice conversation. My mother-in-law said, "I wish someone would have told me it was going to be this hard." This was after already finishing her chemotherapy and during her radiation treatments, during which time she went to the emergency room for an excruciating headache.

I have been inspired to write this book by everyone who has been in a situation in which they feel they are over their heads and are looking to improve their quality of life. This book is for anyone who has had breast cancer and survived it or who is supporting someone in that process. If we work together, the cure will be found for future generations to come. That is why I am donating half the proceeds I earn through this book to charities and organizations such as the Race for the Cure and Fox Chase Medical Center where my mother-in-law is being treated. Although this book is not specifically for patients, any patient can use these practices to improve the quality of their life.

Finally, I would be nothing if it wasn't for my wife. You have been my muse and everything I could have asked for and more. Thanks for always supporting me in any dream I have begun and for letting me know when this book was on the wrong track. You are a miracle for which I am forever thankful for. Your passion for learning has been a model for me in overcoming all odds.

In addition I would like to thank Sandy and Mark from Edit911 for helping me discover the missing links of this book. I would also like to thank Joel Hochman and his whole team at Arbor Books for their guidance and cover design.

How to Use This Book

You will use this book to stop thinking, start living, and begin celebrating every moment of your life by becoming a Renaissance Man or Woman. How will you do this? First, you will read this book with attention. Notice I do not say with absolute concentration or effort. Attention gives an abundance of knowledge, which is not limited by your previous opinions. You will read without concentration, comparison, or forced effort. This will enable you to open your mind to many new possibilities. To practice reading with attention read this book aloud to receive all it has to offer. You will become aware of universal truths, including the law of attraction, which will empower you to practice the seven pillars of strength. They are fun and will bring joy into your life. They have the power to teach you to become spiritual, which enables you to revere every moment of your life.

Change can occur in a moment, and it only takes a week to transform your life. You will maintain this change in the practice throughout your life. Furthermore, you are perfect in this very moment and open to infinite possibilities. You will not just practice for seven days or just the seven pillars of strength because you will add to your practices in infinite proportions with great abundance. It may only take a moment, but you will use seven days to improve the quality of the rest of your life.

Right now declare that you will read this book in its entirety to awaken to the overall picture of your new balance of mind, body, and spirit, which will allow you to live the life you were meant to live. Then you will use this book as a syllabus for the rest of your life. A syllabus is a plan, which the professor composes, so the student will stay on the path to success. It is not absolute but a guide from which at times you may diverge.

After you have read the book in its entirety, you will bring awareness to all you have learned and apply it in your seven-day boot camp to begin the process. You will make a goal to bring your spirituality and dedication, as well as awareness, to the universal truths, the seven pillars of strength, and finally your new dream.

After you complete the seven days, you will continue the practices and repeat this seven-day marathon once a month for seven continuous months. This will enable you to reflect and modify your practices of right thought and positive action in a manner that will constantly draw from the abundance of energy, love, and acceptance in our perfect universe. You will repeatedly set three goals based on the universal truths, the seven pillars of strength, and your dreams. Your dreams will become realities, which will open the door to more abundance than you ever thought possible. These goals may add more time to your practices or further reduce your negative behaviors.

One of the most powerful parts of this book is the additional suggested resources at the end of the book and the related readings sections after selected chapters, which identify the books you will read to increase your awareness of the universal truths and the seven pillars of strength. These books and DVDs have increased my awareness and awakened me from the dream that once overtook me. Throughout the book, the Renaissance and wise men of the past are quoted. These quotes have been set aside to bring your attention to them. When they arrive, welcome them and bring your new awareness to these truths. You may feel compelled to discuss this with friends and family. Using the truths and pillars from so many spiritual teachers described in this book, become a Renaissance Man or Woman. They will change your life as they have changed mine.

You will realize the purpose, which was established before you were even born, of manifesting the abundance of love through the celebration of your life. Affirmations, gratitude, visualizations, goal setting, feeling, and celebration are essential parts of your newly fulfilled life. Right now make your first declaration of your fulfilled life by reading each line with attention, and taking a deep breath after each line allowing the words to fill your body with an abundance of love and acceptance. So, read each line aloud then inhale and exhale and be reborn to this moment.

I declare the truth and give thanks.
I am perfect as I am in this very moment.
I am beautiful, strong, unconditionally loved, and accepted.
I am _____.
And I am choosing to be happy today.

Thank you for this very breath.
Thank you for allowing me to practice.
Thank you for the abundance of wealth, relationships,
and well-being in the world.
Thank you for _____.

I close my eyes and envision
My dream.
I see myself achieving my goal to become a Renaissance *Man or Woman*
And to _____.
I visualize my newly fulfilled life.

I feel
The gift of this dream and my goal becoming a reality,
The one loving consciousness, which flows through our universe,
Full of unconditional love and acceptance
And this abundance of *(God)* energy.

Celebrate.
Smile.
Have fun
and feel the joy of living.
I give thanks for receiving all of this.
I give thanks for my greater purpose and the overall balance in my life.
And I give thanks for _____.

I declare
My purpose, established by
(God, a higher power, or the universe)
Is to spread unconditional love and acceptance through
_____.

I will constantly be reborn to this moment
without memory or judgment.
I will share all my wealth, relationships, and overall well-being
to improve the quality of life around me.
My *(day, evening, or* _____.*)* will be enjoyable and fulfilling!

You will continuously revisit this process before, during, and after completing the practice of the seven pillars of strength, throughout reading this book, and for the rest of your life. You will memorize this declaration (you may call it a prayer or an affirmation) by making it your own and by using it whenever you find old negative thought patterns arising or as you feel an abundance of gratitude in this moment. I repeat it aloud as I drive to work and before and after practicing every pillar. It has brought joy and happiness into my life.

Remember this book is universal. It makes no difference what religion you practice or do not practice. I have attempted to use words that are neutral to all trains of thought and so use love, God, pure consciousness, a higher power, and any other words such as these interchangeably. Scratch out the word I use and change it to whatever makes you comfortable. The words are irrelevant to me.

Before reading any further in this book I would like to make some clarifications over some of the vocabulary I will be using, which unlike the words above have distinct definitions. When you have any confusion over any of these words throughout your reading, please return back to this page for clarification. First, we will talk about the "ego," which is not someone who is arrogant. It is your subconscious mind, and the voice in your head. It is not you who observes the voice but the actual voice that drives you to make good or bad decisions. It can be considered your conscience, but I define it more as your confused subconscious. It controls your thinking at times, and it causes you to lose your-self in your thoughts. This is "incessant thinking," which is when you dwell on a problem in your life. You continually revisit the problem without control, and then the problem magnifies into a bigger problem. It usually occurs during stressful points in the day when you are overwhelmed. Incessant thinking and ego can be used interchangeably in this text because they are that voice that we at times cannot control.

In addition, I want you to think of your mind as consciousness or your thoughts. It is whatever you hear in your head, and again it relates to the ego and incessant thinking. As you become a Renaissance Man or Woman, your consciousness begins to empty. Your incessant thoughts decrease, your ego disappears, and your mind is free.

Consequently, I want you to think of your brain as a computer, it is mechanical. Do not think of it as consciousness or the ego; it is just the machine we use to make calculations. When you are engaged in solving a mathematical problem, you are not incessantly thinking. You are actively engaging in the problem; and throughout this book, I will refer to incessant thinking as thoughts produced by the ego and engaged thinking as when you use your brain to solve a problem. Hence, you are actively engaged in the moment.

Furthermore, a Renaissance Man does not identify with the ego because he does not fall to its incessant thinking. He is engaged in every moment of his life in a spiritual manner through his balance of the understanding of the universal truths and the power obtained from the seven pillars of strength to override the ego. He lives an abundant life because he no longer believes in the lie that he is the ego. Additionally, he knows he is part of the pure consciousness that is the life force of the universe. He is love, he is God, and he is perfect. Therefore, to live the life of your dreams, balance your life

> *For once you have tasted flight, you will walk the earth with your eyes turned skywards, for there you have been and there you will long to return.*
> — *Leonardo Da Vinci*

in a spiritual manner by using the universal truths and the seven pillars of strength to detach from the belief that you are the sinner, a cause of suffering, or the ego. Your goal will be to awaken to this moment with complete attention. Therefore, stop thinking, start living, and celebrate every moment!

Finally, thank you for living a fulfilled life with a greater purpose because that has been my dream. I have continuously made affirmations to ensure this reality, felt gratitude for your enriched life, visualized, set goals for you, felt an abundance of positive energy, and celebrated in my practice as a Renaissance Man for you!

Introduction to the Renaissance Man

Weekends are my days to catch up on talking to my family, and I was able to talk to my sister on this particular Saturday. It was a nice conversation. The fact that I was writing this book came up, and she asked me if I had watched *Oprah* this week. I hadn't. Nonetheless, the conversation continued and Colleen asked me if I knew about *The Secret*. I didn't have a clue; I thought she might be having another baby. I was wrong. It was an episode of *Oprah* that my mom had brought to my attention earlier in the week. Ironically, most of the books I read become *Oprah* books shortly before or after I have read them. This was why I was surprised I hadn't heard about *The Secret*.

While my mom watches *Oprah* (along with most women in America), I rarely do. When I was in high school, this was the only program my mother was ever interested in. My mom is the type of woman who doesn't know how to turn on the television, which gives *Oprah* a lot of credit for doing the unthinkable and making Michelle Walsh watch television. Mom even bought a Tivo to record *Oprah* when she is working late.

I hadn't seen *Oprah* since my last visit to Cleveland over Christmas, and I had no idea what this week's episodes were all about. I asked Colleen what "the secret" was? She explained her understanding of it and said that it all made sense and was obvious. "You know, being positive and positive things happening to you, but why do they talk about this energy thing? I mean, being a science person, it just doesn't, I don't know, it just seems improbable. I need evidence."

Immediately I thought of the conversations years earlier that I had had with a psychologist, Domenico, about choice, meditation, and spirituality. He spoke in this poetic manner about the power of meditation, and it just didn't make sense. I was the doubting Thomas, the skeptic who believed it all to be an over dramatization of what is. I knew it was probably healthy, but it was not for me. There was no way my mind was able to believe all that he told me. I could not comprehend what he was articulating. He tried to convince me to act, but I did not understand this.

I thought reading would lead me out of depression, but he kept insisting I needed to do something. What did he mean by this? I was lost in a sea of confusion, which was shaped by the negative thoughts that consumed my mind. If I would have heard of the secret or any other universal truth in this time of my life, it might have just brushed past me; but I will attempt to teach you what he was trying to teach me.

I am writing this book to those of you who are still searching for the answers but haven't been able to hear the truth because your minds will not allow you to comprehend it. The truth is there are no answers, but there are simple solutions when you open your mind to the truth. I am just an average man, and I have found all of this to be so obscure in the past. This book is an attempt to write in a language that is clear to you. As your mind may be in turmoil and you may doubt the idea of the universe being guided by these universal truths and the power of the practice of meditation, I will use my life as an example of how to supersede these obstacles and acquire what you want, living a life of purpose. As I argued with Domenico that I was not the type of person who meditates, so my wife reciprocated this belief as I tried to teach her of its power.

> *I have been impressed with the urgency of doing. Knowing is not enough; we must apply. Being willing is not enough; we must do.*
> — *Leonardo Da Vinci*

I thought yoga was for strange people who wear even stranger clothes. I was wrong. All the truths and practices in this book are universal, and they see no faces. They are for everyone and anyone. You can begin practicing them in the comfort of your own home without quitting your job, changing your name and religion, joining a monastery, or becoming a member of a yoga studio. They bring excitement and fun to anyone open to their power. They carry with them positive energy and contentment to your heart, and they inspire you to celebrate every aspect of your life.

My problems are of no greater or lesser consequence than yours. I am not a spiritual sage or a wise old man who has an overwhelming amount of life experience. I am just like you. We breathe the same air and think the same thoughts, although now I probably think less and breathe more.

In the past, I was self absorbed. I thought my life was so different from everyone else's. I was blinded by the unconscious ego into believing I could not change or climb my way out of this hell. This is the great lie I will speak of, which most of us are fooled into believing. We believe that there is some innate flaw inside of all of us, and we believe that God is sep-

> *Midway in our life's journey, I went astray from the straight road and woke to find myself alone in a dark wood.*
> — *Dante Alighieri*

arate from us. Unlike the truth that empowers us, the lie makes us weaker and weaker. We begin to feel completely helpless, and finally we give in to all of it. The lie becomes the reality we live in, and we are completely overtaken by the mind. Slowly, through the universal truths, seven pillars, and my increased sense of spirituality, I was able to gain strength and find my way out of this dark path. I began to see the light shining through this darkness. I began a continual rebirth with great purpose to celebrate life and share my abundance.

A whole society had this rebirth during the time of the Renaissance as people celebrated man and the beauty of the universe. They were no longer trapped by the medieval fear of God and the imperfection of man as they had been in the dark ages. People feared death, the hierarchy, and secular powers as if they were all one unified dictator. Before the rebirth, art and intellect were extinct for hundreds of years, replaced by plagues and famine. This was a time that was basically whited out in world history books, and then the Renaissance brought the world back to life.

This process began in my life when I started to practice some of the pillars that I discuss throughout this book, but I still was lost. I tried to convince people that they should do whatever I was doing at the time, and I was still very self-righteous. First, it was meditation, then this book, then that book, then running was the answer, or my religion was the problem. I kept reading and changing and doing, and I had random glimpses of an awareness of the truth. Sometimes those glances would last an hour, a day, or months at a time; but I was never able to maintain them with consistency. I was creeping into this awakening and rebirth as my ego was kicking, screaming, and dragging along the way. I was set off course many times; but every time I realized I had gone astray, I felt that much stronger when I got back on course. Little by little, my opinions were reduced and my ego was overtaken by a great awakening, finally culminating in the process of beginning to write this book. It came in a flash.

After reading *The Secret* by Rhonda Byrne as well as William Glasser's *Positive Addiction*, I realized why I have been able to overcome my depression and live a full life. The seven pillars of strength bring endless amounts of joy to my life. They make me happy, and I feel the great abundance of the world through them. *The Secret* is based on the law of attraction, which states that parallel thoughts, feelings, and actions gravitate towards each other. Therefore, when I was successful in changing my thought patterns and removed doubt from my life, I was able to achieve anything I set my mind to accomplish.

Nature never breaks her own laws.
— Leonardo Da Vinci

I began to think more positively, and this manifested into the reality of my life. The more I practiced these positive practices, the more strength and spirituality I gained, which helped me to continue to grow by empowering me more and more with each new pillar. As the strength increased, I decreased my negative habits. I verbalized, visualized, and expected to achieve what I wanted; and I received these great fortunes with a smile. I was thankful for them, and I shared them with whoever would allow me to. When I reverted to my old style of incessant thinking and negativity, this is exactly what the universe brought to me. There is no trick to be learned. When we are depressed or exhausted, we try to blame it on our jobs or running. If we choose to blame this feeling on running, we stop running, we depress even more, and we forget how healthy running is. Our egos weaken us again and again.

Clear your mind of "can't."
— Samuel Johnson

Most people know their thought processes need to be changed, but they fail to do this because of the complexity of this challenge.

Others try to change their actions but forget about their thinking, which overtakes them. Additionally, there are the spiritually minded people who are focused solely on faith but do not act or bring attention to their thought processes. Actions enable more awareness and strength to empower you to change your thinking. It is imperative that the two practices work simultaneously in partnership with spirituality and for you not to be apathetic in any of the steps to create balance. This will lead to your increased spirituality, and you will begin to cherish every moment of your waking life.

Therefore, you need positive addictions in your life. You need to visualize what you want out of life every morning and, more importantly, during every occasion a negative thought arises. After you have realized the purpose in your life, which was established by what you may call God, a higher power, or the universe, you have the motivation and the strength to achieve anything you set your mind to. The truth is you are beautiful and it only takes a moment to realize how wonderful life is. This is more of a concept than a single idea. We control our destiny through what we think about. If we stop thinking about what we don't want and we make positive affirmations leading to choice, we will look beyond our troubles to uncover the answer. This is what this book is all about: the story of how I, just an average Joe, was able to triumph over my negativity and doubt to become the Renaissance Man.

> *He who loves practice without theory is like the sailor who boards ship without a rudder and compass and never knows where he may cast.*
> *— Leonardo Da Vinci*

Your mind will try to create feelings of emptiness and exhaustion as mine has. At times after running, dancing, or practicing yoga, you may feel depleted. You may become sore or frustrated in your practice of meditation. Do not confuse the causes of these feelings because the practices themselves are the solution to these negative thoughts. You will begin to use the pillars, which are seven positive actions laid out in this book, to counter your mind's attack.

These feelings occur when you are not applying unconditional love and acceptance to yourself or when you become tired because you are not practicing the pillars enough. You will learn how to stop being tricked into just practicing one universal truth or pillar because balance of all will allow for the greatest fulfillment in your life. The two concepts of controlling your thoughts and practicing positive action will become unified, forming one universal spirit. This will transform you into your true self. It is the answer to the question asked in another episode of *Oprah.*

This episode was entitled "Reactions to the Secret." A young woman said she realized instantly what she wanted, but as my sister had said, she felt lost in the pursuit. Many ask how you can put all these ideas into practice. This book is about becoming aware of the universal and interconnected truths that help you to begin to practice the seven pillars of strength to improve the quality of the rest of your life in a spiritual manner. After you have become aware of these truths, you will be born again. Then you will change your thought patterns as I have, and you will set a goal of what you want out of your life.

This may be contentment, weight loss, restoration of health, a better job, an intimate relationship, or more wealth in your life. For example, I have continually set goals of improving the quality of life around me; but the goal is irrelevant to the probability of it taking place. You will continue to visualize and feel as if you have already received this gift. Then you will begin to practice the seven pillars of strength, and not act directly on obtaining this wish.

These practices are direct actions that enable you to maintain your new thought processes and become spiritual. You will make choices through these practices to obtain what you are seeking without effort. They will empower you to continue maintaining this new outlook on life, and they will help you to realize your dreams with purpose beyond yourself. You will write with a pencil, as discussed earlier, your dreams in the line provided and erase them as they become a reality. You will take this abundance of love. Then you will create even bigger dreams that were chosen before you were even conceived to spread this unconditional love, the force of the universe, through your celebration and these dreams. Again, you erase and write new dreams in this book. The abundance will pour into your life because you continually allow it to. You will celebrate this love and success, and the process will continually cycle around. This is only the beginning of the practices that will grow throughout your life. Although this is not the only way to maintain the power of the universal truths, my personal practices have allowed me to be successful in my pursuit of happiness.

My ideas are not original or new. They are a collaboration of different perspectives of how positive action leads to acceptance of who you are. This is a realization of how perfect you are right now in this very moment. This enables you to realize your purpose. When I was truly lost, the books I read had many answers, but I wanted a more step-by-step process. This book is an attempt to create solutions for problems by practicing specific disciplines that will help you as they have helped me break out of the darkness and into the light. My struggle of acceptance began with an obsessive exploration into the meaning of life during a period of time when I was attempting to stop my negative thought patterns, such as depressing and complaining, as well as my drug and alcohol use. My ego made this a slow and difficult process. Finally, after many trials and tribulations, I became aware of these teachings and now practice them everyday of my life.

I am reborn as a Renaissance Man every morning of my new life, and this helps me to realize the interconnectedness of this universe. Therefore, I am aware that we are all in this together. We are not separate from one another; we are of the same line. Perfection lies in the self as we are and in compassion for all. Every moment of your life is a direct cause or effect of everyone else's life. From your toothbrush to your car, you are dependent on the universe to bring you what you need. This enables you to have compassion for all because we need the earth for food, the sun for energy, and each other for everything else. A truly enlightened person is someone who looks into a crowd of people and sees no faces. He only sees a ray of shining light projected through every individual, tree, branch, flower, drop of water, and rainbow. All in this world are transparent and always changing, with no beginning and no end, an endless tapestry of love.

In this book, I will continue to use poetic language to write about the nonphysical and indescribable elements of this world. They can be felt through awareness, but they can't be explained with any true justice of their meaning. Most truths cannot be written with the flaws of the pen; they are too pure to be put on paper. However, I will attempt to converse on what I have found. What have I discovered you may ask? That I was perfect as the child even when I was spoiled, as the adolescent pulled into the conformity of my peers, as the depressing college student, as the confused first-year teacher, as the struggling newlywed, as the arrogant new guy at work, and as I am in this very moment. In actuality, I was not any of these because they are all traits of the ego. I am the awareness and life that runs through your veins and throughout the universe. We are a universal consciousness and life force, although we have been convinced otherwise.

Humanity has been fooled into thinking that we are not perfect, but we are perfect in every breath we take. This has been seen through history; it was apparent in the times before the Renaissance when man despised all that he was. Our unconscious mind has collected dividends on our incessant thinking, although a new consciousness is arriving in the dust. The ego knows that he is against the wall, and that is why there is an explosion of suffering, pain, and war. More importantly, there has also been a sudden increase of consciousness in the world and separation from the egoic thinking. Every day more and more people are waking up from their blind illusions. They are seeing the light shine through the emptiness in their lives. They are realizing the abundance in this world. They know it is free for the taking, and they are beginning to receive it. They are realizing there is an endless supply of anything they could ever want. All they have to do is ask.

We are at a turning point in the evolution of man, and we need to come together to counter the ego, suffering, and sin. We need to awaken to the fact that these are separate entities from who we truly are, and when we stop identifying with the lie. We will be reborn and realize the truth that hate has never overtaken love. This will empower us, because it will enlighten us to the ego's weaknesses. The lies of the ego may be strong, but the truth is stronger. Many have tried to counter this idea, but they have all fallen short. Napoleon attempted to do so, Hitler scared us, Stalin overwhelmed us, Saddam failed miserably, and many others have come along the way. They never last, though; ignorance always falls to compassion. When you fill your heart with love and acceptance, this completely undermines the ego. The ego cannot survive where there is an abundance of love, and there always has been this energy in times of hate. This is why all of these ego driven dictators have failed. It calms my soul when I reawaken to this truth of their lack of success to rule the world. Love is infinite and all powerful.

Therefore, instead of trying to solve the dilemma of incessant thinking through thinking, you will take another path. You will start making positive affirmations using the law of attraction to lead to choices and disciplines that will create balance in your life.

The law of attraction is just as apparent as gravity. We are stars that pull our thoughts into a reality of our creating. Because time is a deception of the mind, we see tomorrow as separate from today and do not realize the power of our thinking. Healthy people around the world see nothing but their abundance of well-being. They draw more positive energy through the law of attraction, and you will too. Nature does not care if you are negative or positive; it just ensures your thoughts become realities. So you will take advantage of this law as so many before you have.

When staring hell in the eye, you cannot fight fire with fire because you are allowing the game to be played on hell's home field. To make an analogy, no war has ever been able to stop war. No matter what perfect cause you may be fighting for, you are becoming just as cruel and evil as your enemy. Once you choose to fight, you become a fighter. You can never claim peace when you have drawn your gun because the gun symbolizes hate and war. Fighting can't stop more fighting. This is the genius of nonviolent protest, which allowed our society to see the ignorance of racism. When the public saw women and children being assaulted by officers during nonviolent marches, there was no evidence to support this unbridled inequality that was apparent in America. The truth was seen on every television in the world, and it demanded our government to pass laws to prevent this unchecked aggression, whether they had planned to do so or not. With Gandhi as Martin Luther King, Jr.'s teacher, he was able to bring this awareness to a country that had been ignorant for too long.

Consequently, we also cannot fight against thinking with new beliefs. We need to respond with action because these practices go past the problem to creating new solutions. Beliefs are one of the most powerful assets of the ego. They are rarely based on truth, but they are a creation of the egoic mind. They are the tool the ego uses against pure consciousness and love. So, if you change your beliefs, you are still not being reborn to the truth. You may have a new belief that you think will crush your problems and the ego, but you are just feeding the ego. When you give it attention, whether it is negative or positive, you are bringing more of the problem. Remember, through the universe's law of attraction, whatever you think about attracts more of itself. The more you incessantly think about something, the faster it will manifest in your life. Therefore, you need to change your focus away from the problem. Although the ego has many tools to overtake your consciousness, you have an infinite source of techniques to choose from to counter its attack.

We have had so many spiritual teachers who have taught the universal truths in their own languages and from their original perspectives. The Renaissance Man tries to learn all these truths to gain a deeper understanding of what is. It may only take one essential understanding to allow your life to blossom, but comprehending all of them will ensure you will preserve this positive transformation. This depth allows greater opportunity through the balance of multiple perspectives of the same underlying truths. When you feel yourself doubting, you can draw upon more inherent strength than you had in the past; and you are not overtaken by the mind as easily.

The Renaissance Man is a program you will use as the roots to the rest of your life. It is essential that you build this program in your own way. The Renaissance Man knows that it takes many paths to find your own. The whole basis of this theory is that we need to practice the seven pillars of strength to become well-rounded individuals as a means to end incessant thinking and to accept our lives in the present moment. You will begin to feel the abundance of this world, and this gives you great power to supersede negativity. Yoga, running, meditation, creativity, and many other practices allow you to feel your inner body, which is this energy more importantly known as love. It is a warm sensation we have all felt and comes in times of celebration and during your darkest despair. This will create the lives we have always dreamed of having through the law of attraction, choice, purpose, and positive affirmations. We will reverence every moment by sharing our unconditional love with everyone and anyone.

Thank you for taking this voyage into the unknown because your new life has been anxiously awaiting your rebirth. Once you begin, your heart will be full and your mind will begin to empty. The sun will be brighter after practicing; and you will laugh, as a child does, without fear or hesitation. You will become overjoyed while practicing and, more importantly, after you are finished. All the pillars have one core element beyond the obvious allowance of love and acceptance. They are all fun! So open the door and step out into your new life. Welcome to the beginning of a breathtaking experience!

I declare the truth and give thanks.
I am perfect as I am in this very moment.
I am beautiful, strong, unconditionally loved, and accepted.
I am _____.
And I am choosing to be happy today.

Thank you for this very breath.
Thank you for allowing me to practice.
Thank you for the abundance of wealth, relationships,
and well-being in the world.
Thank you for _____.

I close my eyes and envision
My dream.
I see myself achieving my goal to become a Renaissance *Man or Woman*
And to _____.
I visualize my newly fulfilled life.

I feel
The gift of this dream and my goal becoming a reality,
The one loving consciousness, which flows through our universe,
Full of unconditional love and acceptance
And this abundance of *(God)* energy.

Celebrate.
Smile.
Have fun
and feel the joy of living.
I give thanks for receiving all of this.
I give thanks for my greater purpose and the overall balance in my life.
And I give thanks for _____.

I declare
My purpose, established by
(*God, a higher power, or the universe*)
Is to spread unconditional love and acceptance through

_____.

I will constantly be reborn to this moment
without memory or judgment.
I will share all my wealth, relationships, and overall well-being
to improve the quality of life around me.
My (*day, evening, or* _____.) will be enjoyable and fulfilling!

Additional Suggested Resources

Byrne, Rhonda. *The Secret.* New York: Atria Books, 2006.
This book plainly and simply has the power to raise you up to use the law of attraction by changing your thought patterns. It opened my heart to my dreams, which have become reality. It opened my heart to new possibilities and has allowed me to feel the abundant energy that floods the universe.

Campbell, Joseph. *The Hero With a Thousand Faces.* Princeton, NJ: Princeton University Press, 1973.
I have always loved stories of heroes, and there is a correlation between all of them. From the myths of the ancient Greeks and Romans to Star Wars, there is an underlining process to transform from the "hero's journey."

Damasio, Antonio. *Descartes' Error: Emotion, Reason, and the Human Brain.* New York: Putman, 1994.

The Feeling of What Happens: Body and Emotion in the Making of Consciousness. New York: Harcourt Brace, 1999.

Looking for Spinoza: Joy, Sorrow, and the Feeling Brain. Orlando, FL: Harcourt, 2003.
If you find yourself needing a more scientific writing on consciousness, these books by Damasio are very in-depth and lengthy texts on the brain and consciousness as science understands them today. He brings awareness to religion and spirituality through his study of the human mind.

Glasser, William. *The Positive Addiction.* New York: Perennial Library, 1976.
This is a great book to read to understand the importance of positive addictions such as running, yoga, and meditation. It has helped me realize why I love these practices but also why at times I have stopped running, meditating, or practicing yoga. This is also where I gained the idea of how to gain strength from these practices to overcome my own

weaknesses by continuing these addictions and increasing my strength exponentially.

Hesse, Hermann. *The Glass Bead Game: (Magister Ludi)*. New York: Holt, 1990.

This book is almost like a real life interview with a spiritual sage. It discusses the meaning of life and the practice of mindfulness. I felt as if I was the one asking the questions. You will get lost in the pages. I wish I could read it again for the first time. It is a page turner you will never forget, and it will answer questions you have never had a chance to ask. Most people never are able to know someone, who is capable of answering these questions.

Krishnamurti, Jiddu. & Bohm, David. *The Ending of Time*. New York: Harper Collins, 1985.

Krishnamurti is one of the greatest teachers of the modern era in this world. He dives deep into where *the lie* was derived and how to bring attention to your life. He has the power to liberate you from all your prior conditioning.

Chapter 1

Beginning Your Path: Understanding the Universal Truths

Forgive Yourself and Others

Life is a wonderful creation. Unfortunately, your mind continually tries to convince you otherwise. The mind persuades us that we have suffered some great pain or wrong doing or that we may have done some unforgivable act that is grounds for others to feel sorry for us. Most of us have some crutch that our mind holds on to, an excuse we give for not pursuing the life we want to live. This crutch is often the result of our own actions or choices or someone else's actions. It is important to become aware of what this crutch might be in our lives and acknowledge it. Then take what has happened and put a positive spin on it.

During the *Oprah* episode, "The Reaction to the Secret," Dr. Michael Beckwith instructs us to reflect on the opportunity that results from an unpleasant

That which does not kill me only makes me stronger
—Friedrich Nietzche

experience rather than focusing on the unpleasantness. To forgive and let go of the incident, one needs to be thankful for the opportunity that arose from the experience (2007).

Previously, I placed blame for my adolescent unhappiness on the emotional absence of my father. He was so consumed by his work and his own agenda each day that spending time with my siblings and I was often overlooked. Now the truth is that, although time with my dad may have improved my childhood, there is no reason why it should have an effect on the present moment. Ironically, the lack of an all-American father provided me with an opportunity to become a very strong person and to love my family unconditionally. As my father's role in our family diminished because of a divorce, the emo-

1

tional void left our family in crisis. Even during this depressing turn of events, I rose above the crisis and gave the unconditional love that my family needed to survive.

All the struggles in my life have done just that. To take control of your life, you need to acknowledge the crutch you're holding onto, forgive yourself and others for their actions, and be thankful for the opportunity to become stronger.

Consequently, forgiveness empowers you to prevent the persuasive mind from making you feel like a victim. Miguel Ruiz described in the book *The Voice of Knowledge: A Practical Guide to Inner Peace* that people often listen to a voice in their heads that repeatedly enforces the idea of being a victim of some action by another (2004). Unlike a victim who is subjected to conditions out of their control, we are liable for our own choices that directly influence our lives. No one has ruined your life or forced you into making bad choices. The mind is polluted. Although it may have coerced you into making those choices, inherently speaking, you chose to become the doctor, lawyer, business man, custodian, salesman, or whatever profession you may be regretting. You choose every day to have a positive or negative attitude; and by choosing anger or depression or closing your heart to new found love, you are liable for your own unhappiness. If you've been raped or abused, that was not a choice you made. However, the choice to think about the situation and to allow it to affect current decisions is determined by you. When you forgive yourself and others, you allow yourself to be accountable and aware of your own choices. This helps compel the mind to make better and healthier choices.

Forgive and Forget
— William Langland

Once you have accepted that your choices alone dictate how your life turns out, there is nothing anyone else can do to prevent you from making your own choices. You may think your situation is beyond repair and that you have hit rock bottom. However, Victor Frankl, who was stripped of his humanity in the concentration camps of Nazi Germany, demonstrated in his book *Man's Search for Meaning: An Introduction to Logotherapy* that he could still choose to have a positive attitude despite his desperate situation (1984). The Nazis took his clothes, belongings, family, and the lives of other Jews; but Viktor still chose to possess a positive attitude. The Nazis, like most people, were completely ignorant to the fact that even in their total annihilation of the Jews, every man could still choose to rise above the destruction. Hence, it is your choice alone whether you live life with a positive or negative attitude.

Attitude is what drives a person's success, failure, happiness, or despair. It may be possible that some people are naturally positive; but for the rest of us, we need to work at it every moment of our lives. I allowed my crutch

> *The superior man is modest in his speech, but excels in his action.*
> — *Confucius*

and lack of forgiveness to cloud my thoughts and control my attitude, making me one of the most cynical and jaded characters you could find. I made Elaine, Jerry, George, and Cramer on Seinfeld look like optimists. Fortunately, I found my way out of this overall darkness through a wise, curly haired Italian psychologist, Domenico, who indirectly saved me from myself without knowing it. Through him, the first truth that I learned was that I could forgive myself and others for actions of the past and that I could tell the voice in my head that said I was an ugly, horrible person and that I hated myself to shut up. Choose to forgive so you can live with a positive attitude.

Accept Yourself With Unconditional Love

Acceptance, which is initiated through forgiveness, is a crucial component of unconditionally loving yourself. Because we are all interconnected, it is as equally important to forgive yourself as it is to forgive others to achieve this acceptance. In an attempt to persuade me to forgive my father, Domineco taught me that if I held a grudge with a family member or anyone I loved, I would not be able to accept myself. My father is an intricate part of me; if I could not forgive him, it was as if I was not forgiving myself. In college, I was able to forgive my father and accept him for the great man that he is. Once I was able to forgive him, I was able to forgive myself, which awakened me to what Eckhart Tolle spoke of as "stillness" in his book *Stillness Speaks*. Stillness is an overall acceptance of all that is in the moment, which leads to a feeling of contentment in life (2003). I felt as though a weight had been lifted off my shoulders and I had been given wings to fly to the highest mountains. This is when I began to love myself unconditionally without fear or judgment.

Unfortunately, without a conscious effort, this amazing feeling of acceptance is difficult to achieve each day. Instead, most people allow themselves to be controlled by their unconscious thoughts, which generate feelings of self-rejection. People reject their appearance, their relationships, their jobs, and most importantly themselves in the present moment. To overcome this rejection, people dedicate their time to jobs and attach themselves to material items in the hope of becoming the best and filling their unconscious thoughts of incompleteness.

> *What spirit is so empty and blind that it cannot recognize the fact that the foot is more noble than the shoe and skin more beautiful than the garment with which it is clothed?*
> —*Michelangelo*

People believe that if they are the best, they will be content and be able to accept themselves. However, satisfaction rarely comes with being the best. Therefore, people continually try to prove themselves through competition and war, which leads to hate and total disarray in society. Our minds are clouded and filled with judgment and self-hate that cause us to reject ourselves and desire to be the best. We can overcome the unconscious mind by the acceptance of all that we are. Remember, we are beautiful, strong, loving, and passionate people; but our minds tell us the opposite. Stop listening to the lies that have left your life meaningless and disjointed and declare your unconditional love for yourself. Look in the mirror and feel that acceptance that your parents gave you as a child held tightly in their arms because that is what we all deserve from ourselves. Without accepting and unconditionally loving yourself, you feel rejected and discontent as you have been conditioned to feel.

Miguel Ruiz explained in another one of his writings, *The Four Agreements: A Practical Guide to Personal Freedom*, that before we were domesticated by our families, traditions, and society, we loved unconditionally (1997). We acted without fear, and we accepted all things as they truly were. Children forgive with no memory, they play without worry, and they run as if there is no tomorrow. Watch children as they create a world without boundaries through their crayons, and you see this lightness of being I am speaking of. As children are domesticated, punished, and rewarded through conditional love given by their families and then by their friends, they fall subject to the mind. Their thoughts begin to bring discontent to their once perfect lives; they fight in the middle of the store for toys or candy and slowly stop accepting themselves for who they are. As you continually fight with yourself instead of accepting yourself, you are as trapped as the child screaming for a key that does not fit the lock of the child's pain-stricken heart. Unconditional love is the only path to overcoming this domestication that controls your thinking.

> *To be wronged is nothing unless you continue to remember it.*
> *—Confucius*

Create Intimate Relationships Without Role Identification

Relationships are what make life worth living. They ensure we live every moment to its fullest potential. If you are not content with your life, your relationships are probably the root of the cause. They are so powerful that when we lack connection with the world around us, we feel alone. We easily identify our relationships with roles that separate ourselves from those who should be close to us.

August Napier, with the help of Carl Whitaker, described role identification in their book *The Family Crucible, the Intense Experience of Family Therapy*. In families and throughout life, we create roles for people. This enables us to feel in control of the world around us and feel at ease. We are caught in the roles that are prescribed by conditioning and time (1978). The human mind categorizes everything and wants the world to stay constant. This is why people naturally like routines; they help people feel they are in control. Thus, we classify and create roles for the people we love; but the problem lies in the process of change. Everything and everyone changes, but we identify with the role they played when we first met them. We are blinded by these roles, and we cannot see the individuals for who they really are in this instant. What do we see? The view we observe is tainted by our past memories of what the person was once like or when your relationship was in great turmoil.

My parents before the divorce played two very strong roles. My father was the unloving and uninvolved complainer while my mother was the wife who would never listen. Neither of these roles accurately describes the wonderful people they both are, but every night the same event would occur. It was the funniest thing because we sat down no matter what was going on and would attempt to have a family dinner every evening. The story was always the same. We would say grace and it would begin. Either my father began to talk about work, asking my mother to listen, or my mother would ask my father to do something. Either way they would set each other off, and what was even funnier was when they did not play into their role. They still would react to each other as if the one had just insulted the other. Without a doubt the conversation would explode into an argument. Finally, someone would leave the table, and then the other. Usually my siblings and I would just wait. Eventually, one would get hungry and we would eat again. This took place for years. My parents knew exactly what to say to set each other off. Neither is to blame because they were not the actual problems. The roles they played dictated the same outcome. The egoic consciousness would overtake our home at the same time every evening. They both worked so hard during the day to give their children all they could; however, they were being fed by the ego and its incessant thinking.

It is easy to listen to the voice in your head, which continuously lies to empower the ego in controlling your life. It comes as a plague that cannot be stopped by any vaccine. It tricks you into believing you are different from the rest of the world and that we are separate entities in a world full of diversity. In truth, we all breathe the same

> *Keep your heart innocent and without memory, living every day anew.*
> *—from the wedding vows of Michael Nardi*

air and are nourished of the same fruit. If I haven't mentioned that I believed the lie, as most adolescents in this country do, that I was the deprived, depressed, and unloved, I will stress this now. I say this comically but we all feel at times in our lives that we have no connection, which is a direct effect of some wrong doing that has been done to us; that no one in the world truly knows who we are; and that no one loves us because, if someone did we would not be negative. In some cases of people who were physically abused or raped, this appears to be more justifiable.

Although I was neither abused nor raped, I felt as if I had been, which I believe is common for most people. The evidence I would have given in defense of this belief is easily proven wrong. I lived through a parents' divorce my senior year in high school. According to statistics, half of the people who get married also get divorced, so this does not put me in any special fraternity. I helped take care of a dying grandfather, but again who has not helped their family members in uncomfortable ways in their times of need. The time I spent helping my mother with my grandfather's sickness I thought was so extreme and that I was being asked to do so much. Again, this is common to the incessant thinking that takes place in society. I also had a father who was not around emotionally, which again is nothing that sets me apart from many people. However, now I have been able to rekindle this relationship by accepting him as he is. After doing so, the relationship flourished. I did this basically by ending the relationship in my mind; I erased all the past pains I felt from him. I attempted to see him in a new light. Like all of us, he has shortcomings yet, at the same time, is an amazing individual. Knowing this allows our relationship to grow continually.

> *To be wise and love exceeds man's might.*
> *—Shakespeare*

I asked what I could learn from this experience, and again I reflected upon the strength I gained from helping my family. Why should I be in pain for his past actions? I made a choice not to allow the past to affect the present. I realized he was not responsible for any pain I was currently suffering; I was choosing to depress. I was drawing the universe to instill more pain in my life. Conversely, I could choose to stop depressing and holding him accountable for my current feelings and begin to love him uncondi-

tionally. I could choose to accept him and to love myself unconditionally as well. My wife and I love spending time with him now, just
talking. He might jokingly say he was a horrible father and husband,
but I have put all of that in the past where it belongs.

My wife and I met on a trip to Daytona when we were building
a house for Habitat for Humanity. Back on campus, we fell in love,
which led to me proposing to her during a carriage ride in Central
Park less than two years later. Most of the time in college, due to my
wife's major, we just watched each other study. I was reading more
and more of the books Domenico suggested, and she was studying
biology. We both were doing our own things, but we were doing
them together. We were intimate because we were both independently being who we were.

As a marriage grows, this is more and more difficult. We are still
working towards getting back to the point where we are both
individuals. *The Art of Intimacy* by Patrick Thomas Malone and his
father Thomas Patrick Malone explains "love, intimacy, and
closeness" in detail. True love correlates highly with intimacy, which
is seeing individuals as they truly are and accepting them without
wanting to change them. Closeness is inevitable in current
relationships and constantly compromises two individuals until they
are breathing and thinking in the same light as the other to make the
situation comfortable. Closeness is caring, which is trying not to hurt
the other's feelings and compromising who you are in an agreeable
manner to be close to one another. Relationships based on closeness
are very fragile because neither person wants to disagree or do
anything that would break the closeness (1987).

Contrastingly, intimate relationships are truly safe because these
individuals accept their differences. They do not attempt to control
what is uncontrollable, which is who they truly are, although at times
closeness is beneficial. I chose to quit smoking to be closer to my wife
before we were married, and that is the most positive aspect of being
close. Quitting smoking did not change the person I was, but it
allowed me to become closer to my wife. On the other hand, if I am
a runner and my wife wants to become one to become closer to me
and she is injured from running more than her body can handle, this
leads to the wrong closeness. This very situation happened last year,
and I stopped running because she was unable to run. Our closeness

caused us to be less intimate. I am a runner and I compromised who I was so we could be closer.

Intimacy is allowing my wife to study to receive her doctorate in physical therapy without distracting her, although I would like to be doing the same type of scholarly activities to be closer to her. When we first met, I began to read more and more so I could become closer to her because she loves learning more than anyone I know. The trick is to be who you are with another person who knows who they are and does not try to change you but accepts all of your idiosyncrasies.

Once you reestablish these meaningful relationships, you need to be gracious for all that has come into your life. You will be forever thankful for this love as these relationships draw upon the law of attraction and continually bring abundance into your heart. Love is fun and it is innocent. It has no ulterior motives; it only wants one thing: Love wants more love. It spreads faster than any brush fire when it is released into the universe. So learn to love with no fear, and take risks in your relationship to share more of your intimate self with another. If you cannot be who you are with your partner and can't even have fun playing in the rain, you haven't found the right person for you. Be thankful for the time you have spent with this person and move on without hesitation.

> *To love oneself is the beginning of a lifelong romance.*
> *—Oscar Wilde*

Love is what makes the world go round, and it is at the heart of all the universal truths and seven pillars. It is the most valuable substance in the world, yet it has no form. It is the nonphysical matter that inspires everyone.

Celebrate by Living Your Life to Its Fullest and Giving Thanks

This simply stated is laughing, crying, writing, painting, dancing, singing, breathing, playing, and enjoying every moment of your life. Life is wonderful! It is meant to be celebrated. That is why everyone loves a wedding. My wedding was one of the all time greats. It didn't cost a million dollars, but you would have thought it had. From the time I entered the hotel three days prior to the ceremony, the two families celebrated our love. Everything was perfect: the beautiful bride, the guests, the wedding favors, the menu, our families—even the rain held off long enough to have the ceremony outside as my wife had always dreamed. That was her only wish for her wedding day and it came true. Even the ultimate wedding cliché, which is the most common reading from the Bible, was perfect. This passage is read in almost all modern weddings because no one, even two thousand years later, has spoken of unconditional love in a more poetic and truthful way.

Love is patient; love is kind and envies no one. Love is never boastful, nor conceited, nor rude; never selfish, not quick to take offense. There is nothing love cannot face; there is no limit to its faith, its hope, and endurance. In a word, there are three things that last forever: faith, hope, and love; but the greatest of them all is love.

—1 Corinthians 13:4-8 KJV

This reading symbolizes the beauty of life and marriage alike. This is why my life is perfect and why the day was perfect: All revolved around love.

There was one problem on this perfect day. The pastor forgot the rings. Yes, we were married, the ceremony was complete, and I kissed the bride. But he forgot the rings. He handled it without missing a beat. We went back to the gazebo and made sure we got it right the second time. It was just another funny anecdote to add to the storybook life I have lived, which my wife and I will laugh about for the rest of our lives.

When you are getting married, everyone has advice for you: some good, some bad, and some just bizarre. At our rehearsal dinner, we were left with advice from a beautiful couple I did not even know. They told us to *never stop falling in love.*

This does not just apply to marriage; it applies to life. Never stop falling in love with life itself. Be like a child. Children live life without fear. They are innocent and playful, and they love every moment of it. They cry one moment, and the next they've forgotten why they are crying and are playing with their friend who hit them. They know what we tend to forget as adults: Life is short. In the grand scheme of things, we are just a blink of the universe's eye. Some fear death more than anything. However, I see it as a blessing. It allows me to live as if there is no tomorrow and to enjoy every breath. Every time my wife and I celebrate our love, it is that much better knowing we are only here

> *If we have been pleased with life, we should not be displeased with death, since it comes from the hand of the same master.*
> *—Michelangelo*

once. Through the love of a man and woman, there is the ultimate expression of this universe—rebirth—which should be your greatest celebration!

You can do this by tapping into one of the most powerful practices in this book. Use laughter as a means of healing as Patch Adams has done. Adams is a doctor who has dedicated himself to improving the quality of life around him. Personally, Adam Sandler has brought so much humor into my life. I love watching his movies with my wife and friends. I celebrate his entire career one laugh at a time. You may not like him, but I am sure you can think of someone that makes you smile every time you hear his or her name. For my wife, it is the show Friends, but whatever it is, is irrelevant to the fact that humor is involved.

> *If a man does not make new acquaintances as he advances through life, he will soon find himself left alone. A man, sir, should keep his friendship in constant repair.*
> *—Samuel Johnson*

Laughter is infectious; use it as a means to draw yourself out of the darkness you find yourself in. Force yourself to laugh when you want to cry. Laugh at all the crazy events of your life. Laughter has the power to cure you from disease and depression; it releases endorphins, which make life a little more fun. It is just one more way to celebrate and give thanks. Once you give thanks, you will want to share all you have.

However, it is apparent to most that all of us have problems in our lives, although I choose not to focus on this. I bring attention to all I have in my life. No matter how bad I feel my current life condition is, I can always celebrate the breath. The breath can be the beginning of these thanks I am speaking of, which you will share with all. Wake up with a smile because you are still breathing. Dance your way into the bathroom and be thankful for this life, which constantly runs through you. Give thanks for anything you can imagine.

For years, my mother has practiced giving thanks for all she has. She has a gratitude book in which she writes all she is thankful for. She reflects upon on all she has been given. She feels endless amounts of love through this practice of giving thanks in life. She taught us to do this through her example. We still pray before every meal, even if we are at a restaurant, by giving thanks for all we have. I now practice this not as she does but during my runs when I find my mind wandering or as I become overwhelmed with joy. As I run, I continually say thank you or give thanks for specific things. I also do this as I am meditating and driving to work. Anytime that I find myself bored, I give thanks. It is so important in life to see that the glass is half full and not half empty.

We live in a time when all our basic needs are provided. It is up to us to accept that our lives are full. Most people have food and shelter as well as love and belonging. If one of these is lost or even if all are lost, you always have life. You have the single breath you take in this moment. This is all you need to be content in life. So give thanks for all of this. What an awe inspiring fact: We all have what we need!

Furthermore, there is an over abundance of wealth in this world. We are no longer fighting for our survival. Even while I was working in the inner city, children had a multitude of possessions; this was not the reality of the past. If you were to ask them if they were poor, they would probably say otherwise. They would brag about their X-Box or new pair of Lebrons.

Love is all you need.
—The Beatles

Now I am not in anyway making the case that there is no suffering in the world. People on the streets are still hungry, and there are many people starving in third world countries. What I am saying is that if you are reading this book, you obviously were able to provide transportation to the store or library to acquire it. You may have not even had to leave your house if you ordered it online. You are probably not lacking any material needs such as clothes or a house, and you are more than likely not hungry. All that is needed is a change of thinking. So become aware of all you have. That is a lot to be thankful for.

I am thankful for many aspects of my life, especially my wife and family. I have not only my immediate and extended family, but also my wife's. I have never been without food, even when my mother divorced my father, because people always ensured our fridge was full. I have always been able to have anything I have desired within limits. I didn't have every toy, but I received almost all I asked for during my childhood and adolescence. I didn't have a car as many of my friends did at the age of sixteen, but my mother helped me buy my own at eighteen. My wife and I have been able to buy and sell a house, and we have always lived comfortably. We have had to watch our spending at times, but we have never struggled like our parents previously had when they were our age. Through their support, we both have been successful and able to graduate from college.

In addition, I am thankful for the trees, the rivers, and endless amounts of life in the world. I am thankful for the truth that so many teachers have taught, beginning with the Buddha and Jesus and continuing through so many other spiritual coaches. I am forever thankful for the guidance I have received from these great minds. They have opened the door to the truth from Eckhart Tolle to Krishnamurti to Miguel Ruiz to William Glasser to many others such as the teachers of the secret. Thank you for sharing your wisdom with me to transform my life into what it was intended to be. Even more, I have been blessed with so many challenges in my life that have strengthened me to become the man that stands before the world writing this book. I am forever grateful for all of this and for all that is to come in the future. Life is so wonderful, and I have such a beautiful one.

Look into your life and see all you have. Be thankful for all your experiences. They have occurred for a great reason. If you haven't realized why, look deeper into the individual event. Start smiling because you are breathing and you are filled with the energy that effortlessly flows throughout the universe. What a magical world we live in where miracles stand before us every day. Wake up from the dream and be thankful for your life. If you want more from it, take it; there is nothing stopping you. There is an overflow of love and acceptance waiting for you in every breath you take. Now, go out and share it with anyone you encounter in your day!

Spread Your Unconditional Love Into the World

This unconditional love will fill your heart and flood into the world. Your friends and family will feel your endless supply of love, and you will be completely content sharing it with them. When I accepted myself for who I truly was with no conditions, I felt manic in wanting to spread my love in any way I could find. I realized that we are the same mind; however, we have been fooled into believing that we are all unique and separate. The same energy that makes up the entire universe makes up your cells; nothing is constant. This energy is always moving. Because it is always moving, we are one endless flow of energy, sharing the same atoms.

> I celebrate myself, and sing myself, And what I assume you shall assume, For every atom belonging to me as good belongs to you.
> —Walt Whitman

Nevertheless, long before there were books, man was overtaken by the idea that humanity inherently is flawed and needs to be transformed into a superior being. All religions have created this idea, whether it is described as karma, suffering, or original sin. The mind has allowed man to believe this lie. This thinking has caused man to attempt to transform into something else. The lie has created a divide between what is and what society believes we should be.

Instantly, there was a separation from the present moment and this belief of perfection that could not be obtained in the present moment. Separation became apparent in everyone to follow, and this propaganda is instilled in every child. In the West, man has been searching for the path to heaven; while in the East, man is trying to end suffering to be in a state of nirvana. Nonetheless, both create a change that has to take place in a person to become more. People work and work to become something more than they are.

The idea of perfection is how the mind never fails to control you. No matter how hard you try, you will never be perfect. Because you believe it is something to gain, you move further from the reality of your presence. Every cell in your body and organism on earth is connected. As you see this, you become aware of the truth. Just being is enough; it is all we ever need. This myth creates the idea of time, which forces a partition from the present to what we aspire to evolve into. What we don't understand is that we are energy, always flowing, having no beginning or end, in the only moment that is right now. There is no real sense of time.

Even worse, the lie has taken form. We cannot differentiate it from the truth. The misconceptions of karma and suffering, as well as sin, have become realities in the present. In Krishnamurti and Dr. David Bohn's discussion in *The Ending of Time*, they ponder where the idea of wanting to become better came from. They found that humanity rejected humanity and started fighting for survival and then began to compete and manipulate itself. The lie grew and grew; people separated more and more from who they were and from each other. Through their thoughts, borders were built, beliefs were created, religions were formed, and

Love more and worry less.
—Anonymous

countries came into place. This resulted in numerous divisions throughout the world. Labels were formed, and this led to the lie that we are all different when in actuality we are all of one mind (1985).

Humanity is of one consciousness, sharing an eternal love that connects us all. There was a glimpse of this awakening during the Renaissance when man began to celebrate himself, which is more of a celebration of our perfect universe. This was short lived until now. We are ready as a universal consciousness to see the truth.

In actuality, this connection is why unconditional love is so infectious. Once you love yourself, you learn to love your neighbor and your enemy alike. You are now aware that there is no difference between you and the rest of the universe. We all worry for our families' well-being, fear pain as well as suffering, and search for better lives. Our beliefs and thoughts that are driven by the lie are the only things that divide us and create this nightmare. When we cease to be opinionated, we love without fear; and we recognize all that is right in the world. We smile and laugh a little more; and we begin to share our love with anyone, even a stranger passing us in the street.

Contrastingly, the time that was once spent with the family is now spent on various distractions such as the commute to work. While most children are being raised by cable television, gaming, and the Internet, most parents desire to have better lives instead of sharing their love with their children. This striving is the direct cause of the problem because parents are not with their children, who are alone while their parents are in their cars or trains on this endless commute. People attempt to use cell phones to feel at ease, but this only distracts them even more. Although children are dominated by their iPods, adults fall to theirs as well, not to mention their Blackberries and their addiction to work. Society has lost the sense of family and community that allows people to have love and belonging. So walk through the streets of your neighborhood and reestablish this through sharing your unconditional love with anyone who walks by. Change your thinking and see each person as another person you can share your unconditional love with.

Finally, spread this unconditional love through giving. This can take many forms. I love to give my paintings to my loved ones, as well as material gifts, my time, a surprise, and my words of inspiration. There is nothing better than seeing someone's face when you have painted something only which is dear to them. I get to see this often, and I think I enjoy it more than they do. I also love searching stores

> Be thankful for small mercies.
> —James Joyce

for the gift someone wants to receive, not that I want to give. I like looking into their dreams and then pulling out something that will enable them to feel unconditional love. It is like listening to their inner desires and showing I have understood by giving the perfect gift to fulfill them.

In addition, since I have moved away from home, I love to give my family time to be with them. There is nothing better than sharing your time with someone. It is the one thing we all feel we don't have enough of. When they know you have sacrificed to be with them, they are forever grateful.

Then there is the surprise. I do this by going to visit someone when I have told them it is not a possibility. My family is known for surprise visits; we do it for each other's birthdays and for special events such as baby showers or wedding showers. I also love to surprise my wife with flowers when I feel gratitude for being able to spend the rest of my life with her. Seeing her smell the flowers and preparing them in the vase warms my heart.

My last gift of giving are my words. I love writing words that empower others or allow others to love themselves. I used to love writing my wife emails, and I still love to write her birthday or anniversary cards. There is nothing better than love letters because there is no better way to spread unconditional love than like a teenager in puppy love. If I ever stop writing them, I will know I need to work on our relationship. Some things just sound better when they are written as opposed to being spoken; they are just more exciting and meaningful. I get excited as I write down the words that describe my unconditional love for Ashley, my friends, and my family.

All these gifts allow me to become much more intimate with the ones I love, and I recommend giving more than you receive. Always try to outdo yourself. I love that my wife always anxiously awaits the gifts I get her. She knows how much thought I have put into them, and it spreads the overabundance of love in my heart into her life. So, if you haven't started giving with abundance, start right now. Write an email or go buy something you know your spouse has been waiting for, or cancel a meeting so you can visit a sick friend. Unconditional love will lead you to eternal happiness right now by surpassing the selfishness of the ego.

Living in the Present Moment

Eckhart Tolle discussed in his book *The Power of the Now: A Guide to Spiritual Enlightenment* the idea of living in the moment by ending incessant thinking caused by the ego (1999). As you are enriched by your acceptance and unconditional love, you are more capable of seeing life as it truly is. Our thinking is what life is; if we choose to think in a positive light, we will live in a beautiful dream. Life is difficult for most, although it does not have to be as challenging as we make it. Your mind tells you how much you have to do each day. Stop it from doing this by creating these new thought patterns. When a negative thought comes in, send a positive one right out into the world. The universe will transform the thought into a reality. Life becomes easier as you make these choices to replace your negativity because you are less controlled by your mind. You are spending less time dwelling on the past. You are moving into the moment of what is.

Contrastingly, many people will lie and create an idea of how easy life could be if they change or buy this or that idea or belief. They are separating themselves from the moment, and this is what makes life so difficult. Everyone has a quick fix—a car, a diet, a look, a fragrance—and we are inundated with endless marketing schemes to continue the lie. Society portrays life as being easy and that we should always be entertained from the moment we wake till the moment we go to sleep. The house, the car, the lifestyle of the rich and famous—they all have one common characteristic: laziness. It can be easy, because your thoughts and not any materialistic idea will bring you to new levels of consciousness. If you are enjoying whatever you are doing in this moment, although it may be a great deal of work, it is less work because of the smile on your face.

> *Kindness gives birth to kindness.*
> —*Sophocles*

As a direct effect, we work more hours in our professions to be entertained, and we spend far less time seeing the moment as it is. If we are more efficient and if we declare what we want to the universe, it will come to us. We are trapped in the past and in what we hope to become, never accepting what we are. Thoughts of past mistakes, future fears, and anything else flood our consciousness with the sole purpose of keeping us from what is. A common error of psychology is to dwell in the past, to drum out painful experiences, memories, and emotions. This leads to feeling pain over and over again without end. Allowing these false memories to control our current lives ensures that we will never be able to improve the quality of our lives. Pain was suffered in the past, and your search to discover distorted memories only causes you to revisit old pain.

The Renaissance Man never experiences the same pain twice because he lives in the present. He is not fooled by time. He is not lost in the past or searching for the future because he understands its truth.

Acceptance of this moment can only occur when we discontinue repeating the same ineffective thought patterns. In a time when there is an influx of meaningless entertainment, overcrowded schedules, overindulgence, and an overall sedentary lifestyle that is wearing away our very existence, we must take back our lives. Our thinking is usually focused on one perspective, our own. We do not see the world as it truly is because every moment is spent depressing, angering, and repressing. Most of our children are being taught to have no will power; they are entertained through their PSPs and iPods no matter where they have to go. If they are at home, they have even more distractions.

As a teacher, I am amazed that any child is able to read at home with all the distractions stimulating their mind. The reason this is possible is because children see that there is more to life than society is portraying. The miracle of school is that these same children who are so lazy at home are able to work eight hours a day with me; some music and my silly antics are their only entertainment in the classroom. However, at home, they sit in front of the television or their gaming systems. There is seemingly nothing their parents can do to stop this. Punishments, discipline, and prodding are all usually ineffective. The only useful technique is coercion, which only leads to more confusion. Then, when the children are bored and discontent with their lives, they fight with their siblings and parents and run right back to the solitude of passive entertainment.

I have seen, as a teacher, how powerful reading is in overcoming entertainment. As my students accept and internalize my love of learning, they overcome their addiction to being entertained by technology. They want to come into the present moment, although most are dreaming away their lives in a false sense of reality that is disconnected to the moment. Even in any of these practices, we can again be sucked into the entertainment that they all can offer. By no means will the practice alone lead to a perfect life. You need to be mindful of the traps there are in all practices by always being in the present moment.

> *The only prison we need to escape from is the prison of our own minds.*
> *—Anonymous*

On a more positive note, society has allowed an influx of different trains of thought and outlets into many different practices previously closed to outsiders. Now the global truths are open to all who are willing to learn through the great teachers of mindfulness, awareness, presence, meditation, and yoga. These practices all lead to a realization of the present moment by not being distracted by the incessant thinking that brings us back to the past.

Diving back into memories of the past that are painful do no good because there is nothing you can change that has happened in the past. In contrast, you can always make choices in the present moment to improve the quality of life. Most of us have minds that dominate our thinking, but some of us do not recognize that they are separate from our true being. This part of your consciousness continually tries to manipulate you into making choices that will allow more ignorance and suffering. The voice tells you to give up because your ideas will never work and never to follow your dreams. It allows the lies of the past to continue to survive in the future. As long as you do not have awareness of the present moment, the mind is winning and your chance at freedom is losing. So rise to the challenge and live in the present moment.

> Time stays long enough
> for anyone who will use it.
> —Leonardo Da Vinci

To do this, you need to be reborn by superseding the ego. There have been three major renaissances in my life when I awakened to the truth. Renaissances take place after the ego has overtaken you to the point where your consciousness has no choice but to break through this insanity. A Renaissance Man continually is reborn moment by moment, but it can take years for others to have a glimpse of this awareness of the now.

The first time this occurred in my life was the last night I ever put an illegal substance into my body. I had hit rock bottom and feared for the life of a friend as we were coming down from our high. As he laid head first into the couch, I fought with another friend, asking for help in finding my way out of the troubles of the current context of my life. I was denied any sympathy or help, and then I awakened to the now. I realized I was the only one who could find the solution to my problems. I was the one in control of my pursuit of happiness. This acceptance was my first rebirth.

The second time came years later right after I graduated and was teaching in the inner city. I was on the floor of my apartment, asking my wife if I could quit. She gave me an opportunity to be reborn by telling me I needed to decide by myself. She told me she couldn't handle my current state. This statement was like a train wreck; it brought me directly into the present moment. It awakened me again to the fact that I was the only person who could transform my life from despair to contentment. I needed to end my self-righteous, opinionated thinking that I was always right, which was driven by my ego. Furthermore, I needed to open up to learning and triumph over my own limited understanding and beliefs.

Finally, after I came to my current job, I again hit rock bottom as I became frustrated with the other teachers because I could not help them or the students in my current position. My ego again sabotaged my awareness and drove me like an arrogant teenager to think I was better than my colleagues. I finally exploded in a way I never thought possible, crying uncontrollably during a private meeting with two principals and the assistant superintendent. Talk about embarrassing, I can't even say it was my ultimate fear because I would never have thought I was capable of this. Out of this devastating experience, I realized what an awesome release it was. My ego had brought me to feel so much self-pity that it was controlling my life. I released any

> *Lord, grant that I may always desire more than I can accomplish.*
> *—Michelangelo*

sense of pride or arrogance when I broke down and cried and came to my greatest awakening. I discovered I had brought this all upon myself through the law of attraction by my egoic thinking. I realized teaching was not what I wanted for my life because I became conscious of the fact that I could not be who I truly was in a school setting. There was a divide because I was not able to motivate, inspire, and help improve the quality of life of millions as it was written. I was driven to write this book and speak out against our present insanity; my practice of the seven pillars of strength would no longer be a secret. I was yet again reborn, forcing me to the present moment.

I have gained so much strength and received so much joy from each of these renaissances. Now I can look back and be thankful for all these opportunities that have returned me to the present moment and brought meaning back into my life.

Find Purpose in Your Life

When I was depressing, I was searching for the meaning in my life that I once had. As a child, I believed it was to be a good Catholic; I was to follow the teachings of the Bible. Then as I realized the world was not as the stories in the Bible had said it would be, I felt lost. When I stopped searching, I realized I had a calling to help others.

> *Be like a solid tower whose brave height remains unmoved by all the winds that blow; the man who lets his thoughts be turned aside by one thing or another will lose sight of his true goal, his mind sapped of its strength.*
>
> *—Dante Alighieri*

Through my experience in a summer camp for students with severe needs, the switch went off. Every day I carried a boy to lunch because he was too tired to walk after we went swimming. I would help the autistic children communicate. Working with the mentally retarded was such an awe-inspiring experience. If they could smile every day with my help, why couldn't I? I was put here, as my mother and all of us are, to help improve the quality of life around us.

Vicktor Frankl found his purpose in the concentration camps during the Holocaust, and he writes about this in *The Will to Meaning: Foundations and Applications of Logotherapy*. Life is not worth living until you have found meaning. This purpose can help you survive the most devastating experiences and empower you to defy all odds (1988). Jesus had the purpose of dying on the cross to forgive all sins, Buddha to search for enlightenment, Gandhi to free India; Martin Luther King Junior spoke of his dreams to obtain equal rights, the Dali Lama to spread love through the world, Jaime Escalante to educate the unreachable, Patch Adams to improve the quality of life around him. What is your purpose?

You may tell me that you have to work in a dead-end job with unlimited amounts of pointless tasks you need to complete and there is no way out. Why are you working there? Are you supporting your family? If this is the case, that gives you purpose. Thank you for giving them what they need.

Children of my generation were sold on the idea that you should have a job you enjoy and, if you work hard, this is a very good possibility. I am not going to debate this, but as I will discuss later in this book, we should be open to all perspectives on an issue. You should have dreams, and you will begin to accomplish them through the understandings you will obtain in this book and the practices of the seven pillars of strength.

This might not happen tomorrow. It is up to you. For now, you need to accept the trivial demands of your job and find purpose beyond your work. See the reality that wasted effort might be given in the process of most of your work days. Dedicate this all to a higher purpose and become aware of your breath while practicing these tasks. This acceptance will allow you to be more content and efficient at work, allowing you to make a change if that is what is necessary. Be willing to do what you may not want to do for the sake of this greater purpose that guides your life with meaning. If you enjoy your occupation and you are supporting your family, this acceptance alone of your meaningless responsibilities will empower you to enjoy life more. So accept and stay or, if the job is too horrible and it is not what you want, move on.

> *Many believe—and I believe— that I have been designated for this work by God. In spite of my old age, I do not want to give it up; I work out of love for God and I put all my hope in Him.*
> *—Michelangelo*

Enjoyment comes through acceptance in life. We begin to find peace in the meaningless tasks of the day. If you choose to look for more out of your life beyond your current occupation, there is another man who can show you where to begin.

Rick Warren inspires followers in his book *The Purpose Driven Life: What on Earth Am I Here For?* to become conscious that we are part of something larger than ourselves. We should find purpose, as he has chosen to teach through his faith, to become a servant of God's teachings. He explains that you are not a glitch in the system; you have been placed on earth for reasons beyond yourself. You are part of a larger family and serve a mission as Christ has done before you. All the turmoil you have encountered in your life has empowered you to become the wonderful being you are today (2002). Knowing this purpose to serve as a vassal of God (the universe or the higher power) motivates you to live a fulfilled life as it was determined before your ancestors were even conceived. You will weed out all that is unnecessary in life, knowing that if it does not fulfill your purpose, it is meaningless and a waste of time.

You may not be a Christian, but you are still aware of how interconnected the world is. A higher power is prevalent in the world. We can find purpose being conductors of this energy, spreading it to all the empty hearts in the world. You need to focus less on yourself and more on others. This will allow you to feel the abundance of love and compassion that are the universal life forces of the world.

Once you have found this purpose for your life, you can become dedicated to achieving your dreams. I was created to awaken others to a balance of the universal truths, seven pillars, their own spirituality, and the celebration of life in every breath. I feel this purpose in every moment, and I allow it to spread through me back into the universe in abundance. You similarly will now make positive affirmations and choices to accomplish all that you have set out to do through the awareness of the law of attraction in serving your greater purpose.

You Are Directly Responsible for Your Happiness Through the Choices You Make

Once you have brought your consciousness back to the present moment and found purpose in your life, you need to reflect on what you want. There are personal attributes that need to be accepted, but there are also choices that can be made to create your ideal life. The best example of something that I have accepted in my life is my big, fat nose. All kidding aside, conformity as a child led me to feel that my nose was ugly. I was teased about it, as many of us are manipulated by our peers because of some attribute they see as a flaw. The truth is, as my wife tells me, I have a beautiful nose; but I used to hold on to the idea that if it was different, I would be better looking. Unless I am so traumatized by my nose that I need to visit a plastic surgeon, I need to accept that it is perfect just the way it is. I use this example because I have an intuition many of your problems are as simple as this.

Consequently, decide what parts of your life you need to accept. More importantly, become aware of the choices you can make within the parts of your life you have the power to change. William Glasser in his book *Choice Theory: A New Psychology of Personal Freedom* examined why we are discontent with life. He found it is mostly because of the choices we make, which directly affect our relationships. You choose to stay in an abusive marriage or in a dead-end job. You could walk away or make better choices to improve your situation, but you choose to depress or anger as a reaction to your negative thoughts and feelings (1998).

> *If you want a quality, act as if you already have it.*
> —William James

Make your body and mind a cohesive unit that is always attuned to your dreams. You are powerful, and you can change any situation when you have complete faith in yourself. No one is forcing you to be discontent in life. Once you realize this, you are not to be reckoned with.

As a teacher, my goal is to help all my students realize they are in command. I cannot force them to do anything they do not want to do. Once they accept this, I also enlighten them to the fact that they must also be in control of how they feel and act. If their day is not going the way they would like it to be, it is because they are choosing to depress or respond to their feelings in a negative manner. They need to make appropriate choices to bring their mindset to a more positive light.

I also help parents by enlightening them to the fact that they do not have to fight with their children over homework. If you want to solve any problem with a child, stop and take a deep breath. There is no trick to fixing your child because you can't fix them. They are perfect just the way they are, but you can help them to make better choices. Put the ball in their court and ask them how they can solve their problem. Most children today do not have opportunities to solve any of their problems because teachers and parents fix any problem as soon as it arrives. Children feel more and more powerless. They acquire self-helplessness because they have been stripped of any responsibility in life. Therefore, empower them to fix their problem of not completing their homework on their own. Give them choice and you will feel free. Choice is so powerful!

One of my students was given this opportunity. He has taken the initiative to wake up more than an hour earlier on the days he needs time to himself. He sets the clock and goes to bed an hour earlier and wakes up to read, play on the computer, or walk the dog. He has gone from being disorganized to being a responsible young man with one choice. He's nine, so imagine what you can do. Choice is all we need because we can choose to accept, to forgive, and to celebrate.

Choose your purpose and choose to make affirmations. They are the key to success and happiness. Every day while I am driving to work, I make positive affirmations. I tell myself I am beautiful, strong, unconditionally loved, and accepted. I repeat these until I'm smiling from ear to ear. Affirmations have empowered me to achieve more than I ever thought possible. Tell yourself every day how beautiful, intelligent, strong, loved, and wonderful you are. I use affirmations when I feel my ego making a strong surge to retake my consciousness. So, when your mind is taking a wrong turn, use this tool to put it back on course. With positive affirmations, you can manifest the life you have always dreamed by exploiting the greatest law that has been in existence since the beginning. It never waivers or goes astray.

> *They can because they think they can.*
> —*Virgil*

As Certain as Death and Taxes

There is only one thing that is more certain than gravity. Like death and taxes, the law of attraction is as constant and predictable as any universal law. There is no way to outmaneuver it. However, you can utilize it to your favor. Make positive choices to ensure your dreams become a reality; verbalize and then visualize what you want. This is not just positive thinking but an actual feeling that encompasses our whole mind and body towards what the universe will provide without question. Build an energy around you that will be a shield against negativity. Esther and Jerry Hicks in their book *The Law of Attraction: The Teachings of Abraham* have spread this idea of asking for what you want from our universe. Once you dedicate yourself to whatever you are moving towards, you will begin to act in ways that make it possible to accomplish your goals. The universe attracts your like thoughts with a reality that is a direct consequence of these thoughts and feelings (2006).

> *If you wish to live a life free of sorrow, think of what is going to happen as if it had already happened.*
> —*Epictetus*

I have been able to do this in my life. As I decided to make the transition into education from my study of psychology, the head of the department ensured me that I would not graduate on time if I came into the major. Furthermore, with my learning disability, I would probably be unable to pass the praxis exams I needed to receive my certification. She basically told me there was no chance of me becoming a teacher and that I should continue the path that I was currently on in the field of psychology.

Driven by my purpose to improve the quality of life around me, I informed my future wife that I would not only graduate on time but I would also lead the major to become the finest teacher possible. I verbalized what I wanted to her, I visualized winning the award, and then I made a dedication to obtain the skills I needed. I continually made positive affirmations that I was a wonderful student and practitioner. Two years later, I achieved all I set out to do and more. I was awarded the distinction of the Presidential Award of Excellence in the field of education. I passed all the requirements for my certification, and I did this all within the time I needed to graduate without delay. That is the power of choice, positive affirmation, and the law of attraction, which leads to actions that directly cause you to accomplish your dreams.

Furthermore, the law of attraction is the secret Rhonda Byrne has thoroughly researched in her book and movie. All the current and past teachers alike explain the concept of the universe responding to your thoughts and feelings. Whatever thoughts are consistently occupying your mind will become the future, and it is up to you to change these thoughts from negative to positive. You choose to create your universe from your fears or dreams. There is an energy that makes up your body, the earth, and the entire universe. It has been defined as the non-physical, love, and God. We are all filled with it, and we can use positive declarations to make any wish our command. Whether you are searching for love, wealth, or anything else, it is all within reach by using your mind to attract it to you (2006).

One of the greatest examples of the power of the law of attraction is the Declaration of Independence. Even in the name of this document, the colonists declared their independence through the use of the law of attraction. They did not hope, wish, or dream for freedom; they outright declared it to be so. Furthermore, they wrote it down. At that point in time, I do not think any one of them knew exactly how they would gain their independence; but once they wrote it in a document, this ended any chance of the British being able to defeat them. The colonists were determined, and I am sure they visualized what they wanted as well. They were more than thankful for the opportunity this would enable future Americans to have, and it became a reality.

> *All that we are is the result of what we have thought. The mind is everything. What we think, we become.*
>
> —*Buddha*

In this moment, I am going to prove the power of the law of attraction. I declare that the culmination of the writings and teachings I have incorporated into this book will find its way into your hands. There are many reasons a book doesn't get published, as you can imagine; but I am erasing them all from my memory. Any time they try to sneak back in, I will think of you holding this book in your hands and feeling complete again. I see the cover with the words Stop Thinking, Start Living, and Begin Celebrating Every Moment. I see that the book is by the Renaissance M. A. N. It is so bright and I can see it is the solution to the problems in your life. Currently, this visualization is making my whole body feel alive with unconditional love running through my veins. I am genuinely excited that your life is changing before your very eyes as you read this book. I want to thank you for this. I am forever grateful for your support.

When I am rejected by agents or publishing companies, this picture of you reading this book, as well as the cover, forms in my mind and the feeling overtakes me again. I send my thanks out into the world for this, and I thank you right now for all you have given me. This opportunity has brought even more abundance into my life, and I think of all the people diagnosed with cancer, like my mother-n-law, that we are helping through the proceeds earned by this book. The law of attraction is powerful, and I am happy I have put these ideas into practice!

Let's say you are as I was, the old doubting Thomas who needs to see to believe. Well, the truth is apparent; it was proven almost forty years ago by two researchers, Robert Rosenthal and Lenore F. Jacobson. The law of attraction has had many names, such as the law of love and many others. Science has its own name for this law; it is called self-fulfilling prophecy and, later, the placebo effect. What we think or perceive becomes a reality. These researchers proved this idea of self-fulfilling prophecy as they explained in their article "Teacher Expectations for the Disadvantaged". Basically, they took a group of children who had no distinguishing characteristics or above average ability and then identified them to the teachers as being highly gifted and hand picked to specifically work with these highly efficient teachers to reach their highest potential. They told the teachers that these children were ready for an explosion of learning and that these teachers were chosen to help cultivate this potential. The researchers expressed how the tests they performed on the children had singled them out, although they were just average students like the control group. There was no difference between the groups other than the instruction that was given to the teachers to help the chosen group (1968).

Anyone who is aware of the law of attraction would predict that the students flourished. They would probably tell you the students had some kind of developmental explosion, that their

IQs shot up through the roof, that the teachers liked these students more and were amazed by the students' intuitive answers. They probably would tell you that the teachers did not believe the researchers at the end of the year when told that these children were just average students at the beginning of the year. They would have been right about all of this. The difference at the end of the year between these students and the control group was phenomenal. As they began they were even, but at the end of the year there was no comparison. That is exactly what the studies proved, the control group made no growth while the others' IQs flourished.

Now think of what you could do with your own life, utilizing what you have learned. There are virtually no boundaries to the potential of your life. We can no longer even say the sky is the limit because there is an abundance of potential that can never run dry. How will you maintain this? You will do so by bringing balance into your life. This will help you to sustain all of your new wealth, relationships, and well-being in your life. It is the glue that will hold all the other universal truths and seven pillars together.

Bring Balance Into Your Life to Maintain Positive Change

I am going to make a prediction that this is not the first book you have read to improve the quality of life. Year after year, people write the universal truths in their books, which empower many to change their lives; but eventually, the flame goes out in your life. Why are we unable to sustain such positive change? We not only have to change our thinking and thought patterns but also have to change our actions in a spiritual manner. How have I managed to maintain all these conditions? I have been practicing disciplines that continually enrich my life every day.

I have ups and downs as many people do, but I have anchors that ensure I will not drift away into the land of negativity. I have found balance in my life that was once plagued by chaos. I have made a positive affirmation that I deserve to live the life I want to live through my daily practices. I continually use the law of attraction to bring more abundance to my life, and I preserve all this through the seven pillars of strength.

These practices strengthen your will and give you awareness of the distractions in your life. Moreover, we do not master any of the pillars, but we become scholars of all of them. This is not a panacea for the current state of society, but a stepping stone to a better life. It might be years before you feel content with your life, or it might be in this moment that all comes into place. It can happen in an instant, but I know it can't happen unless you are practicing passionately. So you need to start now. You have made a very important first step by picking up this book.

> *It had long since come to my attention that people of accomplishment rarely sat back and let things happen to them. They went out and happened to things.*
> —*Leonardo Da Vinci*

The second choice you have to make is to set a goal after you complete this book, or right now, that you will abide by the seven pillars of strength to become a Renaissance Man or Woman. You will bring awareness to all the universal truths, and you will use the law of attraction to obtain all you have dreamed of having. Any person can do this by accepting the inadequacy of their current life. I apologize that this book is written in a male dominated language, but that is only to portray the theme of the Renaissance Man, which was the man who was psychically, mentally, spiritually, emotionally, artistically, and intellectually accomplished. He celebrated every aspect of life and reverenced every waking breath.

Renaissance is a French word that means "rebirth." This was a time in history when there was a great awakening of the mind, body, and spirit. The Renaissance was an economic, spiritual, artistic, and religious revival. Man began to celebrate the beautiful creation, and humanism was created. There was a realization that man was not imperfect. Consequently, there was an influx of celebration of man and invention. Directly prior to this time, the focus was on the flaws of man and on repenting for all his wrong doings. The dark ages were just that, dark and distorted, only focusing on the negative aspects of humanity and the world. Contrastingly, there was a revival, as if God parted the clouds and the sun shone through. The human mind again was free to recreate all that was beautiful through multiple endeavors. They stopped thinking, started living, and began celebrating every moment.

During the fourteenth, fifteenth, and sixteenth centuries, Italy again became the center of the world, having a surplus of scientists, linguists, and artists. Leone Battista Alberti was the first true Renaissance Man; he was an artist, author, poet, linguist, philosopher, and architect. Born of noble descent, he was afforded the opportunity to study in the finest schools; and he continued to learn throughout his life in all different content areas. There were also Leonardo Da Vinci, Michelangelo, Dante Alighieri, Giovanni Boccaccio, and Giorgio Vasari among many others who are quoted throughout this book. Their thoughts are timeless, and they can bring awareness to your life. What beautiful works came from this time!

We are part of another renaissance in this new global and interconnected consciousness of our present period of history. This will be a time of rebirth during the new millennium for all to explore the universal truths and the seven pillars of strength. Specifically, you will experience this process in your life as so many others have. Your consciousness has been waiting for you to awaken from the dream. You will, as many enlightened men and women before you, become well-rounded and balanced in many media, celebrating the utter perfection of the universe. The Renaissance Man balances his life with awareness in mind, body, and spirit because of his consciousness about how fragile life is. He constantly is reborn to this moment through attention and practice of the seven pillars of strength. He has no memory, always seeing what is true without judgment.

Additionally, like a brother and sister playing on a seesaw, he knows if too much pressure is put on one side of the seesaw, it will propel the other up in the air and knock it off track. The seesaw is the spirit that connects the body and the mind. This is why children love to ride together because they can enjoy being in equilibrium (until someone decides to get off and slams the other down to the ground). It requires this equal feeling between the two playmates and the seesaw. They know not to push too hard. If one weighs too much, they give some of their strength to the other. The seesaw provides the rest. They can play for hours as long as no one decides to break the balance. We maintain all positive change through equilibrium of body, mind, and spirit. The love and joy encountered during all the practices of life are infinite with true balance.

The best analogy I can give of balancing in present society is in the field of education where finally there is balanced literacy. This is a culmination of thirty years of research in literacy that has enabled teachers to teach in a balanced manner combining many different styles into one cohesive practice that teachers create in their own classrooms. It incorporates the age old practice of phonics with new practices of guided reading, writing workshop, word study, independent practice, and many other proven strategies. Society loves to swing on the pendulum from one extreme to the other when we could integrate all the proven research practices that have been successful.

Humans need balance. Although many people focus on one theory, I believe we as a people need to incorporate many to invent a new humanity. This may not be an easy path, and I guarantee it will not end in the direction you may imagine it will. I am certain that if you choose to become a Renaissance Man, you will begin to take accountability of your life, your awareness will increase, and your overall quality of life will be enhanced. You will reduce unnecessary activities in your day that do not directly correlate with your new found purpose. Whether this is watching less television or making fewer complaints, you will end such activities, knowing what you know now about your purpose, the other universal truths, and the law of attraction. This is not a quick fix, although it can be; it is not a linear step-by-step process but the big picture of how to have a life worth living, with no regrets, leading to contentment. Serving God, a higher power, or the universal consciousness through your feelings of the energy that runs through all our bodies allows unconditional love to overtake the lie. You will practice these pillars not to obtain anything or for any future gain; you will practice to reawaken from the dream that has overtaken you. Every moment from this day forward will be practiced with awareness of the breath, and you will no longer be overtaken by incessant thinking. Life is too much fun to be bored and depressed now. You will feel love through this new balance, and joy will fill your heart.

I declare the truth and give thanks.
I am perfect as I am in this very moment.
I am beautiful, strong, unconditionally loved, and accepted.
I am _____.
And I am choosing to be happy today.

Thank you for this very breath.
Thank you for allowing me to practice.
Thank you for the abundance of wealth, relationships,
and well-being in the world.
Thank you for _____.

I close my eyes and envision
My dream.
I see myself achieving my goal to become a Renaissance *Man or Woman*
And to _____.
I visualize my newly fulfilled life.

I feel
The gift of this dream and my goal becoming a reality,
The one loving consciousness, which flows through our universe,
Full of unconditional love and acceptance
And this abundance of *(God)* energy.

Celebrate.
Smile.
Have fun
and feel the joy of living.
I give thanks for receiving all of this.
I give thanks for my greater purpose and the overall balance in my life.
And I give thanks for _____.

I declare
My purpose, established by
(*God, a higher power, or the universe*)
Is to spread unconditional love and acceptance through

_____.

I will constantly be reborn to this moment
without memory or judgment.
I will share all my wealth, relationships, and overall well-being
to improve the quality of life around me.
My (*day, evening, or* _____.) will be enjoyable and fulfilling!

Additional Suggested Resources

Byrne, Rhonda. *The Secret.* New York: Atria Books, 2006.
This book plainly and simply the has power to raise you up to use the law of attraction by changing your thought patterns. It opened my heart to my dreams, which have become reality. It opened my heart to new possibilities and has allowed me to feel the abundant energy that floods the universe.

Frankl, Viktor. *Man's Search for Meaning: An Introduction to Logotherapy.* New York: Simon & Schuster, 1984.

The Will to Meaning: Foundations and Applications of Logotherapy. New York: Penguin Books, 1988.
The books have the power to help you find purpose in your life. All his experiences lead you to the understanding of how silly we make life. He was able to survive the Holocaust with his drive and attitude, and you will be able to find your motivation through his books. They helped me to find meaning in my life by improving the quality of life around me.

Glasser, William. *Choice Theory: A New Psychology of Personal Freedom.* New York: Harper Collins, 1998.
Choice theory has the power to make you more accountable for the happiness in your life. You will stop being a victim, and you will regain control over your life. This is a very analytical book, which will help logical thinkers break through to solve their problems.

Glasser, William & Glasser, Caroline. *Getting Together and Staying Together.* New York: Harper Collins, 2000.
Getting Together and Staying Together is a wonderful book to read individually or with your significant other to find your essential needs. This will help you to see what types of love you like to receive, and it will enable you to understand how to love without judgment. You will awaken to your quality worlds, and this will help you to establish relationships that

will last. Glasser has multiple books in addition to the ones mentioned to help you with your children at school as well as during their teenaged years through their teaching of choice theory.

Hicks, Esther & Hicks, Jerry. *The Law of Attraction: The Basics of The Teachings of Abraham.* Carlsbad, CA: Hay House, 2006.
Through the teachings of Abraham, you are better able to understand the law of attraction and how to be more aware of your thoughts to overcome negative patterns in your life. I will admit that I am still taken aback by the introduction of this couple's story, but the words in the book are priceless. They clearly describe the idea of the frequencies we all transmit and how the universe reacts to our thought patterns, whether they are good or bad.

Malone, Thomas. & Malone Patrick. *The Art of Intimacy.* New York: Prentice Hall, 1987.
This book goes in depth into the idea of the ego, closeness, and intimacy. It has helped my wife and I find contentment and acceptance in each other. You will be able to see your friends and family for the wonderful people they are without judgment.

Napier, Augustus. & Whitaker, Carl. *The Family Crucible: The Intense Experience of Family Therapy.* New York: Perennial Library, 1978.
They have helped so many in ending inaccurate roles, which have bound too many family relationships. I have utilized their teachings to improve the quality of my relationships without role identification. It is helpful to see real life examples of families to relate to.

Rath, Thomas. & Clifton, Donald. *How Full Is Your Bucket? Positive Strategies of Work and Life.* New York: Gallup Press, 2004.
These two psychologists have researched the power of positive thought and action in life. It is an awesome book to raise your awareness and excitement of the power of a positive balance in your life. It is a quick read, which I use when I find myself being overtaken by the mind. It will teach the

power of a compliment, among other techniques, to maintain positive thought patterns.

Ruiz, Miguel. *The Four Agreements: A Practical Guide to Personal Freedom.* San Rafael, CA: Amber Allen Publishing, 1997.

The Mastery of Love: A Practical Guide to the Art of Relationship. San Rafael, CA: Amber Allen Publishing, 1999.

The Voice of Knowledge: A Practical Guide to Inner Peace. San Rafael, CA: Amber Allen Publishing, 2004.
Miguel is a Toltec teacher, which means he teaches through the many great prophets of the world in an eclectic approach to allow you to forgive, stop being a victim, find true happiness in yourself, and share your love with others. He will teach the idea of the storyteller. This will enable you to see the truth and falseness of every voice you hear.

Tolle, Eckhart. *The Power of the Now: A Guide to Spiritual Enlightenment.* Novato, CA: New World, 1999.

Stillness Speaks. Novato, CA: New World, 2003.

A New Earth: Awakening to Your Life's Purpose. New York: Penguin Group, 2005.
Eckhart is the forerunning teacher of living in the present moment, the now, by diminishing your ego and not being trapped in past negative thought patterns. He enlightens you to the power of the mind and how to overcome unconsciousness.

Warren, Rick. *The Purpose Driven Life: What on Earth Am I Here For?* Grand Rapids, MI: Zondervan, 2002.
For any Christian, it is the perfect book to discover your purpose, but it also very effective at raising questions for people of all faiths. Rick Warren is clear in the concept of realizing that our life is beyond what we see it to be. There is a guiding force who planned everything to come for you with purpose.

Chapter 2

The Origin of the Renaissance Man and the Seven Pillars of Strength

My Story

Before I go deeply into each of the pillars, I want to give a brief overview how I became a Renaissance Man. It was a path that has taken many turns, but they have been experiences that I am forever grateful for. Your path will be very different from mine because no two are alike. Even as my wife and I have grown together, we each have found our own way. A psychologist and my passion for the truth initiated the beginning of my path years ago, and I am continuing this path as I write these words on the page.

I can feel the love and compassion returning to your body. You are beginning to see the purpose of your life unravel in front of you; and through your positive thoughts and these feelings, you are receiving over abundance from the universe. This is inevitable because of the law of attraction: You ask and it manifests.

Although my path really has no true beginning or end, it began, as yours has, as I took my first steps during the creation of the universe before there was anything, and as it will continue after I have passed on. I hope you enjoy your path as much as I have enjoyed mine. All you need to bring is awareness and these loving feelings of acceptance. You will begin to reverence each moment of the day. All Renaissance men and women are reborn in many different forms. Never occupy your mind with the how; just be thankful, as I am, for receiving all that the universe gives you.

Meditation

My rebirth began as I found meditation, which led to the discovery of the six other pillars. During this time in my life, I began some of the steps of a Renaissance Man. I began to research as much as I could about the meaning of life. More importantly, I began to meditate. Self-acceptance and love are inevitable in meditation as long as you practice with a lightness and sense of humor. Meditation was the beginning of my presence overcoming my egoic thinking. Slowly, it developed into a practice and a major part of my life.

The key is following the breath from your nostrils down to your lower abdomen. The goal is to have an awareness of your thoughts, only watching them rush past you, not indulging in them and being overtaken by them. I began to enable thoughts to come in as waves crashing into the shore, and I allowed them to continue into the undercurrent back into the sea. In the past, my negative thinking caused me to depress by concentrating on all my shortcomings. Then I realized I could replace these thoughts with positive ones. This new frequency transmitted positive energy into my consciousness.

Practicing meditation has endless benefits. The overall objective is to just STOP and sit. We live in such a frantic time we need time to decompress, to alleviate the constant recognition of negative thoughts in our minds, which we follow wherever they take us without contention. They form prisons from which we feel we cannot escape.

I made the error of discussing and defending this practice, which has led to some discontent along the way. I have learned from these errors, which may help you on your path of discovery. Domenico tried to educate me not to talk about it to friends or family until I had dedicated myself to the practice. If you are choosing to begin the process with someone close to you, that is wonderful for support; but meditation is not something you want to bring up for informal conversation at dinner. Domenico knew too wisely that all people fear change of what they don't know and their pessimistic egos tear apart something you have found to be beautiful only because they listen to the voice you have attempted to avoid.

Learning

This process of meditation had the direct effect of effortless learning. Motivation and self-acceptance empowered me not to be distracted by righteous thinking. After I taught in the inner city of Cleveland, true learning began for me as I left my ambitions at the door. I opened up to multiple perspectives on issues on which I previously tended to sway far to the right or left. This type of learning is the next pillar to be discovered; at its heart is innocent questioning. We learn because it is fun, and it keeps the mind moving. When we discontinue growing, the brain begins to atrophy. This is why we should always be discovering new truths.

As children, we learn continuously until we reach school. Then slowly, teachers, conformity, fear, and boredom deprive us of our passions. Math was my passion; I asked questions that could not be answered. Eventually, I stopped asking the questions and gave up on obtaining a deeper understanding. As time passed in high school and college, advisors and professors attempted to lead me into higher mathematics; but I was not motivated or interested in any of this.

Most children in modern classrooms have similar experiences at school. We need to teach reading, writing, research, and problem solving through cooperative learning, actively engaging students in real life contexts to avoid producing apathetic learners. From the beginning of the day until they hear the last bell ring, students should work in groups to help each other learn these necessary aptitudes. Even though we have a disconnected curriculum based on low and irrelevant state, national, and world standards, students are able to rise above any challenge through high expectations and teamwork.

Furthermore, entropy of energy is inevitable when we are not learning; therefore, we need to start. Begin by practicing this pillar as a curious child inspects the world through innocent eyes. Children playfully enjoy learning, so reach back into the curiosities of your childhood and begin the voyage. As we get older, we learn less and less and conform to our beliefs without opening to new ideas. Some stop learning altogether. If they do read, it is only content that agrees with their unwavering opinions. Try to see the other side or to learn something you thought was too difficult to comprehend. If you are motivated, there is nothing that can prevent you from learning. Learn to speak a new language, to draw, or to cook. Experiment with new ideas and start having fun questioning past beliefs. Do not allow the lie of the past to stop the evolution of humanity from reaching a new consciousness. This modern renaissance can't take place without an open mind. So welcome this rebirth by learning continually without fear.

Improving the Quality of Life Around You

This pillar came into place as I was a child, but it did not fully manifest until I was in college. It evolved from my mother's constant modeling. I could not have asked for a better mother. My mom is straight out of a 1950s black and white television show but with a special twist: Mom has cooked, cleaned, and also worked three jobs most of her life. She makes everyone that walks through our door feel at home. She has given all she has without question since she was a child because she knows there is an inexhaustible abundance in the world to be shared with all. By helping her sisters, her mother, my father, my immediate family, and everyone she ever came in contact with, she has drawn upon the universe to provide for every need she has faced. Working to assist her mother, who divorced her alcoholic father, she gave up her savings to help. She had a goal to put all her children through college, which she has nearly accomplished. She created a social concerns group in our church. She has enabled me to help the poor since I was six years old, and we went to church every Sunday. Hence, this has been a direct cause of my goal to work with others. It is probably the reason I became a teacher. Her modeling led to my conception of one of the core pillars, improving the quality of life around you.

I began this through teaching, although my wife used physical therapy as her means. I am an idealist, so just play along. If everyone had a profession that had as a goal the improvement of the quality of someone else's life, we would have a big, fat happy world. Improving the quality of life begins with accepting your life and feeling the universe's endless stream of love and compassion. Subsequently, you will share this abundance, as my mother has with others, by not being controlled by incessant thinking. When you are in this moment, you are better able to help others because you are less focused on yourself. Most people are so self-centered in this day and age; their thinking is consumed with how they can change to make their lives more fulfilling.

In reality, you are perfect the way you are and helping others to realize this in themselves is at the heart of this pillar. The more you spread love into the universe, the more love the universe brings back to you. Your frequency draws this abundance of love and compassion into your life, and a new reality is formed. By accepting and loving your husband or wife unconditionally without judgment, you improve their quality of life.

Spirituality

This pillar is inevitable when you practice the others. As in the humanist movement that took place during the Renaissance, you will begin to reverence all that is beautiful in this world. Beginning with the breath, you will celebrate each of the billions and billions of individual moments that are the framework of your life.

When I speak of this spirituality, I am not pointing to any specific religion because all can promote or deprive you of true spirituality. Religions at their core are beautiful, but the institutions created on their behalf unconsciously have been used for deceitful means. They were the domesticating forces of past millenniums. They were formed to control the masses and to help improve the behavior of man. They lack faith in the perfection of man. They use dishonest means to manipulate the masses into believing out of fear. By no means, however, do I think any of the teachings by the great spiritual teachers that promote love and acceptance have caused any of this pain.

I believe in all religions and none of the religions. You may ask what I mean by this. Let me attempt to explain more clearly. I believe in a higher power, but don't ask me if I am a practicing Catholic, Muslim, Lutheran, Hindu, Buddhist, or member of any other organized religion. It makes no difference what religion you practice. The Renaissance Man or Woman is spiritual and does not argue about which religion is better. He understands that there are many different paths, no one greater than the other. My path has taken many different turns.

I love going to my wife's family's Lutheran church on Sunday, but it probably is for many different reasons than anyone else sitting in the adjacent pews. I like the sense of community and the singing. As a kid, I sang until someone said I had a horrible voice. At this church, I have enjoyed using my voice every Sunday at 9:00 A.M., although I do feel sorry for the people sitting around me who have to listen to me; but they don't seem to mind.

It is apparent that there is something beyond my understanding that drives all life in this world. It can be called God, energy, love, the force, or any other name. It is pure and has no ulterior motives as do the institutions that claim to punish, murder, and exile in the name of God. I don't mean to be pessimistic because my mother's faith has helped her get through more than I probably ever could have handled, but I just don't put too much faith in the institution. I don't think Jesus or Siddhartha, who preached from the sands that God created, would really think all that has been created in their names are necessary. Jesus explained, "if you split a piece of wood, I am there. Lift up a stone, and you will find me there" (GTh 77). God or as I call it pure consciousness is everyone and everywhere. We are part of a collective consciousness, which is this world; and there is nothing spiritual that should ever separate us from each other. Knowing of this connection enables us to put down the barriers that have caused so much pain and suffering.

Running

You may ask where the running and walking come from. Well, there are two reasons, one of which is common sense and the other comes from a great psychiatrist William Glasser from a book he wrote decades ago called *Positive Addiction*. We generally spend most of our lives indoors sitting down. Our ancestors thousands of years ago walked and ran for survival because it is an innate human process necessary to feel complete. The benefits are endless if done in moderation. Naturally, your appetite will decrease and you will look and feel better. Chemically, after you become addicted, endorphins will be released; you will feel a natural high we have replaced with cigarettes, caffeine, sedatives, antidepressants, amphetamines, overeating, gambling, and all of our other bad habits that give us a false sense of comfort. When you become addicted to running, you lose yourself in the run and release the stresses of the day by ending the ego's incessant thinking for at least a half an hour to an hour a day. The strength that is gained physically and mentally need not be mentioned either (1976). I am not talking about getting on a treadmill at your private gyms. Go to the park, the beach, or the woods. Be one with the birds, listen to the perfection of flowing water, and see the overall beauty of something that hasn't been made by man.

This is another pivotal connection you can be aware of, the beauty of nature and the interconnectedness of the world. Walking and running allow you to lose yourself in the utter beauty of the world in which we live. There is so much noise in the world today; to be in a place of peace, such as a park, only hearing running water and the birds, creates stillness, a silencing of the mind. A tree can teach us so much about life: how grounded it is and perfect just the way it stands. A flower need not change; it is perfect. There is so much beauty in the world to discover as you run alone on a beach. It is a meditation in itself to run along a stream just listening. So, lace up your shoes and have some fun.

Creativity

Additionally, the Renaissance Man or Woman is artistic in some manner. I find painting to be my release and contentment when I am practicing what Mihaly Csikeszentmihalyi, a psychologist, calls "flow," a state of mind that completely engages you in the activity of the present moment with no thinking involved (1990). I enjoy painting for Ashley, my muse; she is obsessed with Tinkerbell, which was the first thing I ever painted for her. Children have been my other motivating guides; I love their faces, which light up at what I have created through love.

You may not be a painter, and that is okay. My wife is a dancer; it has empowered her to obtain an overflow of success in life through hard work and dedication. It has given her strength, which all of the pillars do. In addition, I have also found writing to be another outlet; but singing, dancing, or acting has the same effect on people. They are fun, a celebration of the joy of living and the gifts the universe has given you. It gives you a certain lightness of being and an aesthetic eye for how wonderful the world is. When you begin to practice this pillar, you begin to see how ornate and wonderful the world is.

Creating is such a marvelous process that opens your thinking to new levels of consciousness. You are very capable of making miracles happen every day with your brush, voice, or your words.

Share these gifts with the ones you love, and the love will overflow from your heart and into your life.

Yoga

Finally, the last practice of the Renaissance Man is yoga. I have found yoga through my discovery of meditation and my wife's passion of dance. It pulls everything else together; it alleviates stress and gives you awareness in yourself, which is hard to find through any other venue. The key is the focus on the breath and the feeling of the inner body, which keeps you healthier and more at ease. Again, it opens the gates of your mind and allows you to quiet your thinking.

Yoga prepares me for the day. I vary my practices from stretching, abdominal workouts, and Vinyasa yoga to the Yoga trance dance. Many others say Pilates gives the same benefits; I have not practiced it by any means, but my wife loves it. Thai chi also plays into this pillar, if you so choose. All require a spiritual awareness of the body and mind, which brings balance to your life. They allow you to tap into the energy source of this world, rejuvenating your spirits by calming the mind.

How to Begin

How should you go about solving this equation? You need to choose how you look at the world. No longer can you use negative thinking, complaining, and blaming for rational reasons of why you are unhappy in your life. This will only draw more unhappiness through the law of attraction.

This can be a difficult first step; I would be ignorant to tell you otherwise. Clear your mind of any doubt, visualize what you want to receive, feel your life changing, and celebrate this right now with a smile. If you begin to take in these practices, you will find yourself naturally reducing the use of these negative habits. Then with your added strength, you will form your new positive practices, increasing the ones that improve the quality of your life. You will reverence all that you do, and joy will

> *Ninety-nine percent of the failures come from people who have the habit of making excuses.*
> *—George Washington*

overtake you. You will have more fun practicing the pillars than you could ever imagine. This will cause you to reduce the negative choices holding you back from your true self. You will feel the world around you through the inner body, and the energy will drive you to an over abundance of love and happiness.

Once you learn to love yourself, you will realize, as Miguel Ruiz explains in his book *The Mastery of Love: A Practical Guide to the Art of the Relationship*, that you need no other person to find happiness. It can only be found in yourself because the entire universe is inside you. This awareness allows you to be free of anyone who treats you in a way that reduces your self-worth (1999). The multiple thoughts that bring your attention away from the present moment will be reduced naturally without effort. Make positive affirmations and choose to live your life with balance. Become a Renaissance Man or Woman. This is the beginning of the process of your rebirth of your true consciousness.

> *If you want to improve, be content to be thought foolish and stupid.*
> *—Epictetus*

My rebirth took place when I found Ashley as I stopped looking to fill my void. I filled the emptiness with my self-love. I opened up and was not afraid of her dipping in my bucket, as Tom Rath and Donald O'Clifton explain in their book *How Full Is Your Bucket? Positive Strategies of Work and Life*. Their theory is developed on the basis that we all have a bucket, which can be overflowing when we are positive but can be depleted from judgment and criticism (2004). This is another analogy of the law of attraction.

Being positive leads to productivity and happiness, and negativity leads to pain and suffering. Wars have been fought because of negative thoughts. The practice allows you to see all things are love and all is one. There is no disconnect; the mind, as well as the ego as a whole, will always try to prove this wrong. The goal of both is to create conflict so they can stay in existence. If all people found contentment in life, love would roam rampant and hate would be lost with all the dying egos. This is what Jesus saw as Heaven on earth and Budda called Nirvana.

The pillars and love are fragile. If they cease even for a moment, hate and ego will seep out and regain power over you. Constantly visualize your dreams in your mind when negative thoughts approach. This program is only the beginning, and all of this becomes harder and easier at the same time when you lose and regain awareness. The ego is very powerful; it has been creating wars and hatred for thousands of years. It will never give up. However, love and this flowing energy that is abundant in the world are stronger.

> To put the world right in order, we must first put the nation in order; to put the nation in order; we must first put the family in order; to put the family in order, we must first cultivate our personal life; we must first set our hearts right.
> —Confucius

As you learn to use the law of attraction, you will learn how to counter them easily. A drop of love breaks infinite amounts of hate. Knowing this keeps you on guard through the continual practice of meditation, learning, improvement of the quality of life, spirituality, creativity, running, and yoga. This is why it is essential that you practice the pillars as if your very existence depended on them. Bring in the wealth of the world with laughter and joy. The world is yours for the taking to share with all! As Jesus broke bread for millions with only a few loaves, your love will bring contentment to infinite numbers throughout the world.

I am now going to utilize examples of these pillars in action in my life, as well as other people's lives, to show how to take advantage of their proven practice.

I declare the truth and give thanks.
I am perfect as I am in this very moment.
I am beautiful, strong, unconditionally loved, and accepted.
I am _____.
And I am choosing to be happy today.

Thank you for this very breath.
Thank you for allowing me to practice.
Thank you for the abundance of wealth, relationships,
and well-being in the world.
Thank you for _____.

I close my eyes and envision
My dream.
I see myself achieving my goal to become a Renaissance *Man or Woman*
And to _____.
I visualize my newly fulfilled life.

I feel
The gift of this dream and my goal becoming a reality,
The one loving consciousness, which flows through our universe,
Full of unconditional love and acceptance
And this abundance of *(God)* energy.

Celebrate.
Smile.
Have fun
and feel the joy of living.
I give thanks for receiving all of this.
I give thanks for my greater purpose and the overall balance in my life.
And I give thanks for _____.

I declare
My purpose, established by
(*God, a higher power, or the universe*)
Is to spread unconditional love and acceptance through

_____.

I will constantly be reborn to this moment
without memory or judgment.
I will share all my wealth, relationships, and overall well-being
to improve the quality of life around me.
My (*day, evening, or* _____.) will be enjoyable and fulfilling!

Chapter 3

Meditation, Awareness, and a Calm Mind

How I Discovered Meditation

Meditation was an unexpected gift at an unexpected time. The story begins when I was much younger. In the fourth grade, I could not read and I was tested for a learning disability. My teacher confronted my mother, and they agreed upon the help I needed. An angel, Mrs.Romi, a special education teacher, gave me the skills I needed to turn my education around. Her life has been taken by cancer, although her presence lives through the students she taught. I hope that some day I will return the favor by helping raise money for the cure and helping a child overcome the trouble I was in as she did for me.

I went to a college that supported my learning difference and was told I could get more financial support from the state because of my disability. I was tested and my depression was revealed. Because my mother was my sole provider and she earned low wages in her jobs, the government supported my education because of my disabilities. This funding from the state enabled me to continue my collegiate career. To receive the aid, I was informed I had to go to counseling; but I refused medical treatment through any drug because of my lack of faith in them from my past experiences. Medications are rarely useful; they usually only become an unnecessary crutch for those who become dependent upon them. I had previously been on antidepressants when I was seeing an ineffective psychologist who gave me the empowered sense that my family was crazy. He also told me I needed to get away from them as soon as possible. He was correct that my family was crazy, but whose family isn't crazy? The antidepressants did not improve my mental state, and I believe they fueled the depression to suicidal levels.

As an indirect effect of my depression in high school and many other reasons, my mother chose to divorce my father, which was the best choice for all involved, including my father. Furthermore, the psychologist believed in diving into dark waters, and we attempted to reflect on my upbringing. This drove my depression through the law of attraction to reach a pinnacle of self-righteousness and caused me to believe my family had caused these feelings. He crippled me from regaining power in my life, and I created a living nightmare through my negative thinking. This psychologist demanded my father move out and encouraged me to move out of my house as well.

I convinced my mother to end the treatment I was receiving when she wouldn't allow me to move out. Through her wisdom, she put her foot down and told me I would be on my own for college if I chose to leave. This ultimatum was such a blessing; because of the relationship we had established throughout my life, I was unable to choose to move out. I could not remove my mother from what William Glasser in his book *Choice Theory: A New Psychology of Personal Freedom* calls our "quality world." This is the world we create, a mental snapshot, which has all that we want in it. When a relationship ends, you usually move someone out of this picture (1998).

During a discussion with my advisor, I was given the name of a psychologist to call who had helped her son. Luckily, his schedule would not allow me to work with him, and he referred me to a man in his office who would change my life. I went to that psychologist the first day, and I was completely honest about my life, which intrigued him. He could not understand the American binge drinking and partying that took place on campuses. He later became a mentor to me; but at this time, I just filled him with every story of my high school and college career of over consumption of substances and stupidity to impress him. I arrogantly spoke of my success in school, and how I was able to manipulate any situation. I spoke of all the indiscretions in my life that had led to no true relationships and loneliness. I was so lost at the time I did not realize what I considered hell and created through the law of attraction by my negative thinking was actually paradise once I turned the light on.

This led me to develop a relationship I had never had with anyone because this psychologist was the first person I was ever honest with. He helped me turn my life around slowly because it took time for me to take the process seriously. At one point, he saw my bluff and called me on what we were really trying to accomplish other than trivial conversation. This is when the process really began, and little by little the darkness faded away as I increased my positive thoughts and actions.

This created a positive reality that led to joy in my life. Slowly, I made choices to improve my life with his guidance. I chose to listen to the voice in my head far less and to be more positive. I made choices that were better than my previous decisions. I accepted myself more and more and finally began to relinquish my ego slowly. This was proof that although change can be sudden, it takes time to have lasting effect. The progress awakened me to a rebirth; I took responsibility for my life. He led me to reading such great minds as Antonio Damasio, Augustus Y. Napier, Carl Whitaker, the Dalai Lama, Eckhart Tolle, Herman Hesse, Gabrielle Marquez, Jiddu Krishnamurti, Jon Kabat-Zinn, Miguel Ruiz, Mihaly Csikszentmihalyi, Patrick Thomas Malone, Shunryu Suzuki, Thomas Patrick Malone, and Viktor E. Frankl.

Through Domenico's guidance, I rose from depression; but more importantly, he introduced me to the gift of meditation. For two years, he tried to convince me to stop, just sit, and breathe. I thought he was absolutely crazy. He had not meditated since his earlier years; and his desire for me to visit a monastery, sit all day, and not talk was beyond my understanding.

You may have similar thoughts and doubts about the process now. You may be filled with the fear that I once felt; this is the ego-based thinking that blocks true awareness. It allows you to doubt any new idea that does not coincide with your current belief systems. You need to take action, which is different from changing your thinking or reading.

Domenico was aware of positive action, which elevates your awareness. Furthermore, he talked about the benefits it would lead to. It would also be a nice weekend away, he joked; but he prodded repeatedly. This discourse took place over a year of treatment and discussion during which I chose to keep my unwavering beliefs between this idea and the truth. Then he stopped pushing and I began!

I love to talk, as you can see with this book. His thoughts of meditation went against everything I believed. How could anyone improve their life by just sitting? This made no sense; knowledge is the way to self-discovery. The Western way is mind and power to rise above the frustration and inadequacy of life. I could read my way into enlightenment by reflecting on the meaning of life.

The usual process began with Domenico suggesting a book that I would read and could not wait to discuss. I remember talking to Ashley before going and telling her this was going to be the meeting I discovered the truth. I believed there was an external knowledge to be found that these writers had and Domenico could share. Consequently, I read dozens of books he suggested with very similar ideas, which are the foundation of this book; but I still was arrogantly driven to believe it was possible to think my way into enlightenment.

I have reread many of the books multiple times. The more I read, the more I realize how asleep I must have been. I had no true awareness of these writings; I was missing the truth that was written between the lines. I was trapped in the words and the thoughts in my mind. I did not realize the writers were trying to put into words that which is too abstract. I myself again am attempting this, and the words are limited in this endeavor. The nonphysical and universal truths lose some of their power in the writing, but it is the tool I am attempting to use to break through this unconsciousness to awaken you to the present moment.

When I realized that I needed to change something in my life, for a reason I am unaware of, I stopped. Then it happened; I sat and I can't tell you why. I felt more alive than I had ever before. Stupidly, I tried to figure it out. I tried to read to discover the truth about meditating. I discussed the process with Domenico to gain more insight, and he even hypnotized me to the point I almost could not come out of it without coercion.

Finally, after sitting over six months, I realized that there was nothing to figure out; you just sit. Wow! I know it goes against the American way. How can you solve anything by doing nothing? What a hypocritical statement! The Eastern way seems so overplayed and ridiculous.

I know the speculation going through your head: Why, how, and when would I have the time to waste on sitting? There are many beliefs and theories about why you should meditate and how it may bring you to enlightenment or, in a simpler manner, reduce stress. I am not going to debate these facts or tell you that you will become an evolved being and reach self actualization. I will tell you this: My mind was overwhelmed with a residue of pain and confusion. Thinking and reading both had their limitations to any further growth. I needed to act. The reading was a start, but it was not until I began to meditate that I felt the real change in my life.

If I can compare my awareness then and now, I would compare the former to unpacking a box of tangled wires and the latter to unpacking nicely folded clothing. I have moved twice in the last two years to locations over twelve hours apart both times in opposite directions. I was in three different school districts in three years, and I have been able to transition because of the strength and stress reduction of meditation.

My wife and I chose to move to Atlanta to be in a warmer climate and, more importantly, for an improved quality of life. Job opportunities in Cleveland were scarce, and I wanted to teach a younger age with a fresh start. My wife was finishing her master's degree and did not know what direction her career needed to take. So it was a mini quest to find ourselves without the distraction of our comfortable lives with our families in either of our hometowns. This was a great choice in our lives if you think of Joseph Campbell's research on the hero's journey in his coveted book *The Hero with a Thousand Faces*. He describes a process of the archetypical hero who leaves his home for some great adventure, to overcome some trials and a great adversity. Then returning back home to improve his society using what he has learned, his strength, and new found wisdom he has obtained (1973).

Meditation helped me to begin this quest. The best example of this journey is in *The Lord of the Rings*. Our lovely hero Frodo, who was a Hobbit, left his home, the Shire, unaware of the path ahead of him on a quest he did not understand. With the help of other great men, he was able to overcome all odds, including all the evil forces that hunted him. Throughout the process, he struggled with himself and with the power of the ring. Then he became stronger as his quest continued, and he was able to destroy the ring that had the power to destroy all that was well in the world. Finally, he returned to the Shire, reborn as a more complete man. Well, there was no ring, but we grew in great depth.

By no means are my wife and I heroes. The idea is that you leave a place of comfort, accomplish something in a place where you are out of your comfort zone, and then you return as a new and more complete person. We bought a house and worked in unfamiliar environments. Ashley discovered what she wanted to do for the rest of her life: We were starting a business, the Sandlot, that encompassed all that is in this book. Then we realized family is really what matters in life. The time you spend with them is the ultimate gift of love, and we wanted to make sure we gave it to her mother in the time she needed it the most. The business and our dreams meant nothing compared to sharing this unconditional love. A better life is not so great if you do not have good relationships. This was when her family needed us most, and we needed to meet this challenge with a smile.

During this time, meditation kept my life at rest and helped me filter out the fear of all the challenges that stood before us. One day while Ashley was making waffles, the phone rang. I saw it in her face before she could verbalize her emotions. In that moment, I decided we were moving and that our life would take another drastic change. My mother-in-law was diagnosed with cancer the day we were to sign our loan papers for the business and a five-year lease for the building, The Sandlot, was to inhabit. Our direction needed to change in a moment. I decided before my wife put down the phone in tears that we were moving to Philadelphia. This was one of the hardest choices we have ever made, but it was the easiest as well. We bought a "for sale" sign to put our house on the market. We tied up the loose ends of the company and settled our losses. However, we did not suffer any real loss when you think of the learning and growth we obtained from researching and creating our company.

We had a beautiful house complete with everything any wife could dream of, including the kitchen, hardwood floors, the great room, the master bathroom (which was bigger than my current bedroom in our apartment in the Philadelphia area); but it lacked one characteristic that all great homes have. I loved my home I grew up in: the smell, the furniture, and the general feeling as you walked in the door. My wife's parents' house still has this quality, which most new houses lack. My only grounding was my practice of meditation and my wife Ashley.

Magically, we packed the house, sold it, and found a job. Ashley was accepted into her doctoral program, she received the scholarship, and we found the perfect apartment. And boom! We were in Philadelphia.

The one thing I forgot to do was to pack neatly and concisely the box of wires to the computer, telephones, cable, and other electronic devices. When we opened it up, it was a mess; everything was stuck together. You could not see where one cord ended and another began. They weren't labeled and it looked as if I had just dropped them all in the box. During the twelve-hour trip, the box was shuffled around in the moving truck until the cords were a jumbled mess. On the other hand, my wife and her sisters folded and packed the clothing in boxes. Everything they packed was arranged in such a way that we had no problem unpacking in an organized manner.

My mind before I began my practice of meditation was like that box of wires. Slowly but surely as I continue to practice, my mind is more organized and a little more efficient. The problem with the box of wires is that when you are moving, you are not thinking about the effect not being organized will have in the future. Your mind is in so many other places. However, if you took the time to pack nicely, when you arrived at your final destination, unpacking would be quite easy. This is true of life. When you sit and meditate, the process begins structuring your life in an organized fashion. There is a place for everything, and you know the quickest way to get to what you need. Your synapses in your brain will fire in perfect alignment. You have more control, being more resilient, to overcome the great challenges that occur in all our lives.

Our minds are so inefficient in their current context; they are the tangled wires that have no beginning or end. Work takes longer because of the worries and negative thoughts that encompass your mind. When you are supposed to be completing a report due in an hour and you have procrastinated finishing it, you think about what your wife asked you to do, the consequences of not completing the report, the beach, the fact that you gave up on your dreams or missed your child's first word, and a million other things irrelevant to the report. So, begin to unwind the box of tangled wires by starting to sit with intention.

The Proven Power of Meditation

In a study of health care professionals, researchers found job burnout could be reduced by decreasing psychological distress and increasing self-compassion with mindfulness-based stress reduction practices.

Shapiro et al, 2005

Analogy: What Meditation Is

Meditation begins like a boring Saturday afternoon in front of the television. For years and years, our egos allow us to turn on the television and just sit trapped in the past. You might be a flipper, which my mom despises; the constant chatter in your brain is like the obsessive pressing of the channel button, cycling through the channels to find something. Not committing to any show, you jump around like a two-year old does, lacking true attention, moving from one toy to the next. On the other hand, you may be the person who is locked into a show or movie that caught your attention for no reason at all. As the movie gets worse, you are even more entrapped, needing to watch it until it ends. No matter what you may need to accomplish that day, you cannot turn off the television. Even after you have stopped flipping through the channels or the pointless movie has ended, you feel less empowered to get off the couch.

You fall back into one or the other—the flipping or the watching—as your boredom turns into depressing or binging on some snack you have found in the cupboard. Instead of walking away and beginning the day, you find your way into the fridge or to another reality television show, which is far from actual reality. You can't overcome this boredom. Finally one day, you realize the utter insanity of this boredom; you begin to paint, run, or work out.

In meditation, we learn to stop being tempted by our thoughts. We end obsessing over the negative ones, and we stop jumping from one to another without control. The awareness from meditation begins with this discovery of the foolishness of being overcome by our thoughts, bringing them into reality through the law of attraction. Then slowly, as you practice, you reduce the times you are fixed upon the television. You start making positive choices and actions forming a new light in your life, allowing positive energy to gravitate to you. At last, you discover the reason for the boredom, which was your lack of engagement in life. With this new wakefulness, the strength of the ego is reduced and your attentiveness is amplified. You are reborn!

Meditation is a direct source of power to cease the continuous thinking generated by the mind. As you develop your practice, the goal is to stop and watch the thoughts in your mind like a cat playfully watches a storm. You attempt to see the storm and then begin to see the individual raindrops without judgment. I was so easily overturned by thoughts that flooded into my consciousness I followed them wherever they took me. As I began to meditate, I became aware of thoughts as they came into my consciousness. Then they naturally passed unlike previously when they would draw my attention away from the present.

I am not telling you that I achieve this throughout the day with no error, but I can say my awareness has increased. My practice travels down a windy road, and my mind regains power even for months at a time. However, as I practice more, I am more aware of the instances when this occurs, which empowers me to stop this from constantly happening. My mind has less and less control over me. Every time I regain the awareness, it is that much stronger. Bring a smile and playfulness to the present moment, and you will never fail to sit in this awareness.

The practice is a form of unconditional love and acceptance of the self. There can be no judgment of the practice; just sit in stillness. The first time you meditate, you are perfect just as you are in that moment. Nevertheless, the last time you meditate, you are perfect at that moment. You may be improving your pose in your mind and body; but this is really irrelevant to the other benefits. The practice itself is of the utmost importance, and it needs to be seen in a light and playful manner. What is more innocent than being with yourself, embracing your fears with love and awareness with a sense of humor? You need to laugh about the process because, if you do not, your ego will sabotage it. Without love, your mind slowly and forcefully takes back control of your consciousness. Meditation can be manipulated by the ego into a time for incessant thinking, corrupting the practice. Be aware of this and create a universe of your choosing.

Beginning Your Practice

In one of my favorite modern action drama movies, The Last Samurai, Tom Cruise is told by a young but wise Samurai that he is thinking too much. He needs to have "no mind." He is practicing with the sword and failing miserably; but when he clears his mind of the people, of the sword, of his opponent, he is able to overcome his mind's distractions (Koyamada et al, 2003). This is the simplest description of meditation; it is taking out the garbage twice a day. Meditating is "no mind"!

What do you have to do to begin this process? First, as in all the other pillars, you need to make a goal or plan. I will meditate for five to thirty minutes twice a day. You can do more. If this is possible, great; but for the rest of us with limited time, I recommend a daily practice of at least fifteen minutes. You have a few choices if you are like me and not naturally flexible like my pretzel of a wife (who danced her whole life).

The Proven Power of Meditation
During treatment of transplant recipients, mindfulness-based stress reduction and meditation decreased negative sleep and mood symptoms
Gross et al, 2004

Buy a meditation bench on eBay or try shavasana (resting pose). If you look on eBay, the benches are wooden and cost from $20 to $100. They are six to eight inches tall.

How do I use the meditation bench? When you sit on it, you put your feet under the bench between its legs; half of your bottom is on the top. You kneel as erectly as you can. You want your spine as straight as possible.

Why should I use a bench? I used to kneel with two or three pillows under my butt before I realized I could buy a bench. The bench helps you to elevate. Using a bench immediately improved my comfort, and I felt more at ease with my meditation. I strongly suggest benches for the average person.

If you are less mobile, you can meditate sitting in a chair or lying in your bed. If you are flexible, you can cross your legs, resting the outside of the foot on the top of the adjacent thigh, which is lotus pose. Really, all these poses are irrelevant for the average person; they are like choosing between a BMW and a Lexus. They are just details unless you are an expert. Don't try to be an expert, although you may be compelled to learn more; just sit. If you are motivated to gain

Lotus pose

Meditation bench

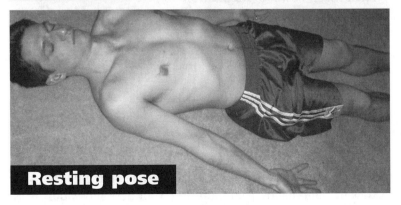

Resting pose

a deeper understanding of the practice, there are many writers I will suggest you read to learn more.

I think the most practical books I have read are the works of Jon Kabat-Zinn: *Wherever You Go, There You Are: Mindfulness Meditation in Everyday Life* and *Coming to Our Senses: Healing Ourselves and the World Through Mindfulness*. Kabit-Zinn is the creator of mindfulness-based stress reduction, which is used by terminally ill patients and others to reduce the stress in their lives. This has led to the multiple research studies previously mentioned. You can find his guided meditation which will enhance your meditation at www.mindfulnesstapes.com. For more guided meditations you can listen to Deepak Chopra's *The Soul of Healing Meditations* and one of his many books on CD, *Magical Mind and Magical Body*. I have found them to have great power in bringing more awareness into my life. He is a medical doctor, who is also using mindfulness to improve the quality of life. The Dalai Lama is also another great spiritual leader in meditation and in life, as seen in his book *An Open Heart: Practicing Compassion in Everyday Life*. He guides you through a world of suffering into a state of compassion you can share with every sentient being. There is also Krishnamurti's *The Book of Life: Daily Meditations with Krishnamurti* and Shunryu Suzuki's *Zen Mind, Beginner's Mind: Informal Talks on Zen Meditation and Practice*, which I read before and after I meditate. All of these can help with your practice, but you can start without reading them.

The Proven Power of Meditation
After eight weeks of a mindfulness meditation-based program in Germany, reduced psychological problems and an improved quality of life were seen in the sample.

Majumdar et al, 2002

The Scaffolds of Meditation

I will now break down the process into scaffolds that guide your practice. If you follow the simple directions I will give, you will begin your practice with ease. Although I suggest any of the poses, I recommend choosing a pose that is most comfortable for you. You should find one that is not painful at all. If you do have back pain, just lie on the floor or your bed with your hands palms up and your feet hip-width apart, opening outward. While in the rest pose, it is easy to fall asleep. However, you want to resist this temptation because it defeats the purpose. Remember, the goal is to become aware, even though it is relaxing.

After you have chosen your pose of least resistance, focus on the scaffolds of meditation. They are not as complicated or strange as you may think. First, close your mouth in a gentle manner, with no force or strain, while keeping your chin down to help you stay awake. Make sure you do not clench your teeth.

Meditation is used to reduce stress and incessant thinking, not to create more. Then put your tongue on the roof of your mouth, touching the upper edge of your teeth. You do this for two reasons: 1) you are going to be breathing through your nose and 2) it allows the neck and jaw to engage in an active rest.

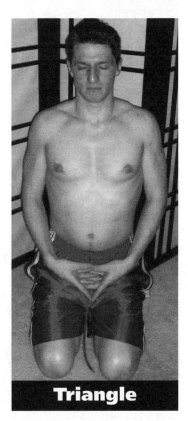

Triangle

Second, you will belly breathe, following your inhalations and exhalations through your nostrils into your body. This is the anchor that will not change throughout your lifetime; your breathing is the one constant in your practice. To bring awareness to my practice and help calm the mind from wondering, I mentally verbalize the words inhale and exhale as I breathe. To do this, inhale deeply. Feel the breath as you continue it into the lungs and down to your stomach. It helps to picture your stomach as a balloon that fills as you inhale, pauses in the stage of nothing, and deflates as you exhale. Again, while you take in a breath, your stomach should expand outward. You pause; and when you exhale, you push it out like blowing your nose lightly. The pause is emptiness, which creates stillness.

Heart Center

Third, you need to place your hands in a mudra, which is a hand motion. It can be as easy as resting your hands palms up or down as you sit. This scaffold helps ground you in your practice. The hand positions are comforting during times of restlessness. I make a triangle by touching both thumbs and index fingers together. Then I intercross my remaining fingers. I rest my hands on my lap as well. Again, if you are lying down, place your arms close to your body and keep your palms up. If you are in lotus pose, you can choose any of these hand positions, as well as placing the palms up on each knee or making circles with your index finger and thumb. With the latter of these choices, you place your hands on each knee with your palms open. You may also see people placing their hands together palm to palm at their heart center, but I find this difficult to rest in throughout the practice of meditation. While addressing all these scaffolds, you always want to be comfortable. Never sacrifice comfort for a pose, which will allow mind and ego to control your consciousness.

Fourth, try to make your posture as erect as possible. This can be strenuous at first because of previous tendencies to slouch, but the health benefits are endless. Push your shoulders back and your spine up. You want to pull yourself out of your waist, elongating as much as possible. No slouching. Good posture helps your breathing; and as you gain more strength, it will allow for greater awareness while meditating. When I have good posture, my abdominal muscles feel stretched, my chest feels as if it is sticking out, and my shoulders are pushed back. As my wife tells me, make sure you don't overcompensate by arching your back when you are trying to move your shoulders into their appropriate placement. You want to be as long as possible, but do not sacrifice your concentration for the idea of the perfect posture. It is a guide in the practice, not a necessity when beginning the practice. It is easy to get lost in trying to perfect your pose, contradicting the fact that you are perfect just as you are in the present moment.

Fifth, relax into all this and slowly you will begin to center your mind on the inner body. I will try to define the term "inner body," which is very difficult to put into words. It is a feeling that is warm, tingling at times; an overall connected awareness with your body and the energy of the universe. Before I began this process, I felt my inner body with my wife as I kissed her for the first time. You feel weak in the knees, your heart is about to burst, and you are totally content in the moment, feeling your body as if it is alive. I find the hands to be the best part of the body to feel first, but it may be different for you. A silly analogy that helps me to feel my inner body is thinking of Star Wars and the force. As you may know, in the movie there is a life force in everyone that Jedis are able to feel and draw upon for unimaginable strength and awareness.

Now that you have some understanding, try to feel your body and begin to attempt body scans as you lie down in resting pose. The body scan is where you feel your inner body with intense awareness of all its different parts. A body scan begins at your feet usually; and then moves up through the legs, the core, and up to the head. You can move from one part of the body to the next. To help propel this process if you are struggling, clench and tighten the different muscles you are attempting to be aware of. Then release. You will feel them.

I only recently mastered this process, although I was readily able to feel my hands and feet. As I

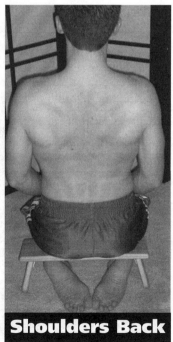

Shoulders Back

attempted to feel other parts of my inner body, I was unable to feel intently as I did with my hands until I read Rhonda Byrne's *The Secret*. Now when I am very aware, my body radiates the energy throughout the universe, overflowing into my heart.

Finally, end every session of meditation with two practices: 1) your visualization of your dream and 2) your bowing ten times to the earth. After meditating, your mind is clear and fresh. Take advantage of this time to visualize what you want out of life. This is the perfect moment to see all that your life will be. Feel your inner body and the wonderful warmth from receiving what you have asked for. Smile because you have done it, and now give thanks for all this love you have received. Share this abundance with the rest of the world because there is an endless amount of this unconditional love and acceptance. Bow ten times to all that you are thankful for. Every time you bow, think of someone you are thankful for or bow to the

The Proven Power of Meditation

In a study of the mindfulness-based stress reduction program, meditation was used with cancer patients and was proven to decrease not only depression and anxiety but also disorientation and aggression.

Smith et al, 2005

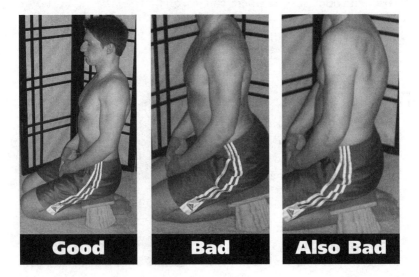

Good   Bad   Also Bad

universe, God, or the higher power in all of us. This brings humility into your heart. Use these two practices as a celebration of life every instance you find yourself meditating formally on the bench or informally in a traffic jam.

Bringing Awareness Into Your Life to Calm the Mind

Meditation is a natural tool a Renaissance Man or Woman uses to be reborn to the present moment. This will lead to an awareness that calms the mind. As your practice progresses, you will be sick less and you will feel revived. I find the morning to be a good time after completing my yoga practice, then again either after work (if I am not running) or right before bed. Again, do not try to think about it or analyze it. This is why I suggest you don't try reading too deeply into it while beginning the practice. When you are ready to move to the next step in meditation, you will know; there is no perfect feeling you should have or culmination for the practice. Consistency is the most important factor.

The goal is to clear the mind, but you do not want to force thoughts out of your head. Redirect your attention to the scaffolds of meditation as a means to become more mindful or to bring positive thoughts into your mind. When you are aware of your mind wandering (and it will constantly try to), refocus on the breath and the inner body. I find that as I meditate more, the placement of the tongue, mudras, and overall posture become innate and improve naturally after establishing this practice. I am constantly mindful of the inner body through my awareness of the breath. As you are drifting into your thoughts, regain awareness by addressing another scaffold. Do not fall prey to the mind's distractions.

> **The Proven Power of Meditation**
> *Stress reduction, better sleep, and a positive mood are direct effects of meditation in the treatment of illnesses.*
> *Carlson and et al, 2005*

Begin the process today. Pick a place in your apartment or house that is away from the commotion of the day. Find some calming music if you would like that, and set up a schedule of when you will meditate. I find it essential that you begin each morning with meditation unless you use writing or yoga as your beginning pillars of the day. Grab your cell phone or an alarm clock, set the amount of time you have chosen, and begin to focus on any scaffold of meditation.

You will struggle with meditation at some point in your practice. I tell you this because I want you to continue the practice even in times of turmoil. Your major focus should be acceptance, not if you are able to accomplish success in the scaffolds because they are only guides. Keep practicing twice a day. Some find the evening is the perfect time to decompress and separate work from home. I enjoy meditation before bed to erase any tension that may find its way into my sleep. Good luck!

I declare the truth and give thanks.
I am perfect as I am in this very moment.
I am beautiful, strong, unconditionally loved, and accepted.
I am _____.
And I am choosing to be happy today.

Thank you for this very breath.
Thank you for allowing me to practice.
Thank you for the abundance of wealth, relationships,
and well-being in the world.
Thank you for _____.

I close my eyes and envision
My dream.
I see myself achieving my goal to become a Renaissance *Man or Woman*
And to _____.
I visualize my newly fulfilled life.

I feel
The gift of this dream and my goal becoming a reality,
The one loving consciousness, which flows through our universe,
Full of unconditional love and acceptance
And this abundance of *(God)* energy.

Celebrate.
Smile.
Have fun
and feel the joy of living.
I give thanks for receiving all of this.
I give thanks for my greater purpose and the overall balance in my life.
And I give thanks for _____.

I declare
My purpose, established by
(*God, a higher power, or the universe*)
Is to spread unconditional love and acceptance through
_____.

I will constantly be reborn to this moment
without memory or judgment.
I will share all my wealth, relationships, and overall well-being
to improve the quality of life around me.
My (*day, evening, or* _____.) will be enjoyable and fulfilling!

Additional Suggested Resources

Hagen, Steve. *Buddhism: Plain & Simple.* New York: Broadway Books, 1997.

Steve Hagan really writes in a simple language in a quick read of what meditation is. The book describes the basic tenets of Buddhism and how to bring awareness to every moment of your life.

Kabat-Zinn, Jon. *Coming to Our Senses: Healing Ourselves and the World Through Mindfulness.* New York: Hyperion, 2005.

Wherever You Go, There You Are: Mindfulness Meditation in Everyday Life. New York: Hyperion, 1994.

Jon Kabat-Zinn, who has been running a stress reduction clinic for terminally ill patients through his mindfulness-based stress reduction program (MBSR). Kabat-Zinn gives the overall picture of meditation in an in-depth and researched based explanation in these two books. He draws upon his own studies and the past teachers of meditation.

Krishnamurti, Jiddu. *Krishnamurti to Himself: His Last Journal.* New York: Harper Collins, 1987.

The Book of Life: Daily Meditations with Krishnamurti. New York: Harper Collins, 1995.

I use his books to center my practice of meditation, reading individual excerpts after meditating. His writings and teachings have so much power I feel I benefit from reading a little at a time. When I was still stuck in the dream of my own creating, he shook up my thinking. At times, he feels so dark; but as I become more aware, he brings calmness into my heart.

Suzuki, Shunryu *Zen Mind, Beginner's Mind: Informal Talks on Zen Meditation and Practice.* New York: Harper Collins, 2001.

Not Always So: Practicing the True Spirit of Zen. New York: Harper Collins, 2002.
These books have excerpts you can read one at a time before or after meditating to gain greater depth and understanding of the practice. He is a very compassionate teacher, and he is playful in his writing. His teachings have great power to center your practice.

The Dalai Lama. *An Open Heart: Practicing Compassion in Everyday Life.* New York: Little Brown and Company, 2001.
His Holiness writes about life and meditation to improve the quality of all our lives through compassion and a cessation of suffering. He has won the Nobel Peace Prize for good reason. His wisdom of the Buddha and compassion will empower you to spread this love to all sentient beings.

Chapter 4

Learning: A Guide to Self-discovery and the Truth

Effortless Learning

When you are motivated, learning requires no effort; it flows naturally. Motivation has been the root of all my successes. When I was young, I needed a good reason for something as simple as tying my own pair of shoes. I found out that when my big brother Billy, my hero, tied his shoes for the first time he got a toy. So I asked my mom to show me, and I got the toy the next day. When I was in preschool, I could care less about knowing the names of the colors until I was not able to play a game that involved knowing this information. That night I made my mother teach me all the colors. The next day I was able to play the game, and I probably won. I believe the reason I never learned to read probably did have something to do with my learning disability, but it had more to do with lack of motivation.

I had a spark of interest in learning when I was a freshman in high school. I went to the top Catholic prep school in Cleveland, Ohio. I had a wonderful history teacher and another inspirational reading teacher in the ninth grade who taught me to learn independently. The history teacher, who is a famous teacher at the school, showed me how interesting the world is and how fun learning can be. He used humor and insight to teach the history

> *Learning never exhausts the mind.*
> *—Leonardo Da Vinci*

of the world, and he has probably inspired thousands of students. The reading teacher was genuinely interested in his students, and he taught me how to study. Most of my learning at the collegiate and graduate levels is thanks to those two individuals. They gave me the motivation I needed to begin to learn, without effort, more than I ever thought possible. This spark caught fire years later in college where the environment was ideal for this type of learning.

Our Discovery

My wife and I have found the perfect learning environment. This Borders Books and Music was in the dreariest town in America, a little city best known for its bad weather. This Borders was wonderful because the coffee shop was off to the side; it was never bothered by browsing customers and was usually full of students from a local medical school. The servers were wise and knew that learning was taking place. We sat there for hours, never interrupted unless the servers were bringing us more hot water for our tea, although they were always ready to make conversation if we were taking a break. They usually asked what we were reading or commented on the book they had previously read that was in our hands. On Friday nights, musicians played, usually piano music, which enhanced our learning. If you had a question when searching among the shelves, it was as if the employee helping you had been searching the topic you were trying to find for their entire lives. If they couldn't find you the book or a good book on the particular topic in question, they took it as an insult to themselves. We haven't found a bookstore like that in any of the other places we've lived.

> *The noblest pleasure is the joy of understanding.*
> *—Leonardo Da Vinci*

However, we have found a nice restaurant and coffee shop, Cosi's, where the servers again are intrigued that we stay all night. When they find out my wife is working on her doctorate and I am a school teacher, they want to know more and encourage us to stay as long as we like. Their excitement is a direct cause of learning because it is contagious. This is another proven example of the law of attraction. We have also found a local Starbucks and Barnes and Nobles that gets the job done when needed. As long as we find a place where we can hide away where there is no coffee traffic engaged learning occurs. So get started and don't be discouraged along the way. You will at times feel as if you are driving in circles, but forge ahead and you will prevail.

The Current State of Education in Society

To understand why most people don't practice this pillar naturally, we have to look at the trend of schooling, which hasn't really changed in hundreds of years. Yes, there are scholar practitioners who use research-based best practices; but overall most learning is factual. Teachers model through the use of textbooks or if they are up to date they use the standards, and students regurgitates the information on the traditional Friday tests as well as the standardized test at the end of the year. All the students have done is memorize facts, which are irrelevant to the real world. No active engagement or "flow" has taken place.

Education in America is static and follows the lowest standards. There are many causes for this annihilation of the current system. One solution that could solve all the problems in the classroom is teaching students how to engage their brain in finding a solution. I had a high achieving third grade class in an affluent school district. When I gave them a word problem for homework, you would have thought I had asked them to clean the toilets from the expressions on their faces. When asked why it was so difficult, they answered, "There was no textbook." "How can we do it if we don't use the textbook to show us?" Don't get me wrong; it was an abstractly written problem, but nothing they or their parents did convinced me that they were unable to solve the problem.

I then opened the discussion to the question of whether they would rather have their brains or a calculator. They were young enough to know that their brains were of more value. (Although earlier in the year, I had asked an advanced fourth grade class the same question; they wavered back and forth between a person and a calculator.) I convinced those children that day that they were bound by nothing and no problem stood a chance compared to their ability to think to solve it.

This idea of engaged thinking I will call active engagement; it is not to be confused with incessant thinking. The word "thinking" is only used to help direct the idea in a recognizable term, but this is when your attention is driven without distraction. You are completely entrenched in the present moment. Contrastingly, while you are incessantly thinking, you are observing your ego's thoughts. You are not engaged in whatever you are working on; there are distracted thoughts arriving into your consciousness. You have no control of these thoughts.

Furthermore, Renaissance Men realize how important it is to challenge themselves. One of the greatest challenges of the modern era is that there are no survival needs for most people to overcome. We are bored. There is nothing on cable, but we continue to watch. People who realize this look as if they have endless amounts of energy. They aren't on the couch; they are continuously learning new things.

The Four Components of Learning

There are four essential components of engaged learning: motivation to find the truth, openness to all views, hard work, and fun. My classroom is enjoyable not because I have some grand skill but because I open the door to what is. Using music and laughter and knowing that people enjoy working hard, I allow students to discover the fun of learning. People naturally take pride in putting enormous energy into something they are motivated to achieve. When they accomplish more than they expect, they feel even better.

I incorporate the ideas of the seven pillars of strength into the classroom, and I educate the students on how to take control of their minds. I accept nothing less than their best, and they love creating quality work. They read and write in their homes out of the excitement gained from their present success

I am still learning.
—Michelangelo

during the day. They build upon these accomplishments and are enthusiastic to learn more. This is why all four components of learning play hand in hand; when you are motivated, you are open to new perspectives while working hard to achieve new success, which is fun.

Motivation

The reasons I have been successful as a teacher begin with my understanding of motivation. One of the universal truths drives this point when we understand that we all need purpose in this life. You need to discover what brings meaning to your life. My job as an educator forces me to ask this question every day when planning how to motivate my students. I use positive reinforcement to teach my students; the more I move away from negative responses, the more success my students obtain. All people love sincere positive feedback. They will work hard for anyone who will give them this while they are completing projects that give them purpose.

Motivation began with humanity's pursuit for survival. It has evolved into so much more. The reason there is so much discontent in the world is because many people lack motivation. In the past, most people were only motivated by their fear of God. Additionally, civilizations that fought for their freedom found motivation easily. Then there was motivation to fight for the beliefs of your country. However, you may not be driven by any of these.

Consequently, you do need to believe in something. If you don't, you need something that sparks your interest. If you are not learning, you are slowly dying to conformity. I am still young in age; but as time passes, I realize one thing: I know very little in the grand scheme of things. The more time I spend in this beautiful place, the more I realize how much there is out there that I have yet to learn. I have been a successful educator because I know I need to continue always to learn more efficient practices. The scholar practitioner always questions how to improve the classroom. I constantly look for new, innovative, and effective teaching strategies I can include in my day.

Finally, this pillar is one of the most important because it benefits the practice and knowledge of the other pillars. You need to learn new things continually or you will become stagnant, closed-minded, and complacent. How do you do this? You do this by always listening. If you begin to feel too strongly about something, investigate the other side of the story.

Openness

If you can open your mind, you will discover the truth. You can only find yourself when you open to all perspectives, new and old. It is critical to have a career that always evolves with the times. Reflection is necessary in any field, and people who tell you that their way is the only way are ignorant. In college, I took a course that was, in a sense, a debate forum about psychological issues at the time. I only took the course because a 400 level class during my sophomore year would look good for graduate school, although I came to understandings that had far more beneficial effects than I ever thought the class would have. Every week we would read two articles from a text that took opposite sides of an issue. I never read; I was too arrogant at the time and thought I had too much on my plate. However, I learned more from that class than many others for which I read endlessly.

How could I learn so much? Many of the issues were deep-seated for many. I, for whatever reason, took no interest in either side on most, if not all, the issues. What I did do, though, was show up to every class and challenge the people who were the most adamant about one side of the given issue. The more strongly they felt, the easier it was for me, the one who was not emotionally attached to the current discussion, to draw the attention of the other students to agree with whatever side I was now defending. My counterparts were unable to look at the truth of both sides because they believed they knew the answer. They debated the wrong points because they passionately felt they were right. They left out key factual evidence in their favor by defending irrelevant opinions. I realized that we are blind to the issues we feel the most strongly about. I played devil's advocate by contradicting everything they said.

This is when I began to form the concept I spoke of earlier because this balance of all perspectives is so essential. I realized that most issues had points too valid to be right or wrong and that it depended too much on the situation to pass objective light on the general

> *Don't judge anyone until you have walked in their shoes.*

issue. My uncle reminded me of this wise saying to follow whenever I pass judgment on someone:

Life is not as simple as we assume some issues to be. There is no right or wrong; everything depends on the context of the present moment. This has helped me realize a great deal about the world. For true learning to take place, you must be open to all views. The truth is so obvious when opinion is extracted and reality shines through.

Subsequently, most people are unable to learn when they are afraid or angry, and this is a great lesson to learn as an educator. The modern classroom is full of children who hate school because they feel they have no chance of success. Just as many adults have given up trying to learn how to change their negative habits because they feel it is impossible. Other students are full of fear; they do not feel safe within the walls that contain them from 8:00 to 3:00. Whether they fear their teachers or other students or they believe they are inadequate, all is irrelevant. The fear causes learning to cease;

> *Difference of opinion leads to enquiry, and enquiry to truth.*
> —Thomas Jefferson

students begin to listen to their minds' irrational thinking. Their daydreams allow them to fly away into a better day, and slowly they learn to remove themselves from the present moment. They are overpowered by these thoughts as they revisit constant pain in their lives. Good schools are safe; their students are aware of their self-worth and the subject matter they are being taught, just as Renaissance Men and Women do not allow fear to prevent their learning.

We need to be catholic not in the institutional or religious sense of the word but in terms of its root definition, which ironically means "open to all." That is why prejudice leads to so much hatred. Subjectivity leads to pain and suffering.

Being open to all races, ideas, concepts, and religions permits humanity to realize the truth. Hate breeds hate and love overwhelms all. It is time we start loving ourselves. Once we accept ourselves, we are able to accept our families and friends. Then the miracle arises: We begin to love our enemies as ourselves, and we break down the walls of bondage that divide us. We are able to share our fears and, more importantly, our dreams with all this abundance of love, which naturally spreads throughout the world because of the law of attraction. It manifests into the perfect universe of your own creating.

Work Ethic

We need to realize effort (which is somewhat misleading because it creates the idea of forced concentration) gives purpose to our lives. I will refer to this as the work ethic, but this phrase is deceiving because when you are driven, it is truly effortless and naturally enjoyable. In *The Quality School: Managing Students Without Coercion*, William Glasser addresses the issue of the work ethic. When children produce quality work, they are proud of what they have accomplished. They are unable to produce quality without spending time on whatever project they are completing. When we work hard towards something we are motivated to accomplish, we feel a sense of accomplishment. The flaw of most modern classrooms is the work that most students are asked to do is at the lowest standard and irrelevant to their lives (1998).

If people knew how hard I worked to get my mastery, it wouldn't seem so wonderful at all.
—Michelangelo

Knowing this, I create projects in which students are engaged and which require them to work harder than they have every worked before. The smiles on their faces after completing any of these tasks are priceless. If more parents realized this from the day their children are born, they would allow them to fail more. This creates turmoil, which leads to growth in a child. The strength obtained is the foundation of their future work ethic.

My little brother Nick is the perfect example of someone who understands the importance of the work ethic. He is a savvy young business man who is about to begin college. Like all of my siblings, my brother has a learning disability; but he still has been able to achieve high standings. With great struggles in elementary school, he repeated a grade and received the skills he needed. He also received additional tutoring from his teacher during the summer. This was the beginning of his devotion to life. It was a problem he faced, which allowed maximum growth. Subsequently, he has become a scholar at one of the most prestigious schools in Cleveland. He is dedicated to success in the classroom, and this is apparent not only in his grades but also from the comments made by his teachers.

Furthermore, he is a hard-working individual outside of school. He has had a job of some kind for as long as I can remember; those jobs have given him purpose. Most teenagers lack this meaning; that is why they make irresponsible decisions to prove themselves. During the summer, Nick usually works three jobs, and he doesn't miss a beat. He is a premature work-a-holic because of the sense of accomplishment it enables him to feel. He also has investments through his earnings that he buys and sells in the stock market through the help of my stepfather Bob's modeling. I look forward to seeing what great works he will produce in his lifetime with his sense of work ethic.

> *Genius is one percent inspiration and ninety-nine percent perspiration.*
> *—Thomas Edison*

Glasser also discusses in the *Quality School* the idea of quality based on the theories of Dr. W. Edwards Deming, who created success in post World War II Japan by teaching his theories to companies to create the highest quality products at the lowest cost. Through team work and collaboration of the leader with everyone in the company to put the product and the work ethic above the rest, they have accomplished much. In contrast, American cars were based on the cheapest cost; and quality was never considered. Now we all know what has happened: The American car industry is falling faster than a speeding bullet, and foreign cars have cornered the market. We need to be efficient and work hard; this will lead to a greater product. The work ethic produces quality. Once you have quality, there are no worries for the success to follow (1998).

Fun

My brother-in-law Mike is a perfect example of a person who realizes how much fun learning is. He is constantly motivated to learn new skills. As a chemical engineer, he has to learn constantly and create new technology. You would think that would be enough. However, every time I have ever seen Mike, he has a new project he is working on for himself or someone in the family. The first time I experienced this was when he was putting in a car stereo. I commented that it was great that he was taught to do something like that. He explained he had never been taught by anyone; he looked it up on the Internet.

He has endless stories of his googling to solve electronic problems. He built his own screen for his projector to save hundreds of dollars, and he can't wait to buy his first house so he can put in a theater in the basement. His new challenge is to make an arcade game from scratch. He bought a book and received the tools for Christmas. He is going to build the frame and then build a computer that will be programmed to have all the old arcade, Atari, and Nintendo games in the system. He knows how much fun and how valuable learning is, and he shows this in all his new exploits and adventures.

> *The great man is he who does not lose his childlike heart.*
> —Mencius

Recently, he and my sister had one of the most beautiful babies in the world, Anna Katherine. As I was watching my niece, who has the largest and most inquisitive eyes in the world, I realized how innately fun learning really is. You can see her constantly learning through her focus on the new world she has encountered. She is learning to roll over, crawl, walk, and all the other firsts. I can see the new synapses in her brain firing like the grand finale of a Fourth of July show. It is the constant, exponential growth that takes place in her young mind. Learning is naturally fun for babies, and it is what they enjoy most. Everything they do is learning. We need to learn as they do, through those inquisitive eyes. They are always open to new experiences, and they smile through every one of those novel occurrences.

The Practice of Engaged Learning

How does a person practice this pillar? The answer is easy: Discover what interests you. This will directly lead to a better understanding of who you are meant to be. With the aid of the other pillars of improving the quality of life around you, meditation, running, spirituality, creativity, and yoga, a person naturally reflects upon who they are. This leads to discovery of what you want to do. Once you find that, you are motivated to learn. Once you are motivated, you will work hard at what you are interested in and you will enjoy doing so.

The seven pillars of strength are what I am constantly motivated to learn more about every day. I have a love of psychology and the mind; I want to improve my teaching strategies, as well as my knowledge of the world in a general sense; I want to strengthen my relationships; and most importantly, I want to improve the quality of life around me. These give me ample avenues to study, although they are different from my wife's love of the workings of the body. We both enjoy each other's dedication to what we each find important. I challenge you to discover and learn about something you are passionate about. Expand your current perspective past the chains that previously bound you.

The most ironic and sad aspect of our society is that most people do not have an urgency to learn. We take for granted the fact that any book is a library away or any topic is a google away from our finger tips. Contrastingly, I have friends I met in college and as a teacher who lived in third world countries during their childhood and never had libraries close to them to access. My best friend's wife, who is from Zambia, explained how much easier it is to learn here with the quick access to materials.

Putting learning to practice involves finding what interests you by answering four questions: What did you like to investigate as a child? What interested you in school? What problems are you having that you want to solve? What is something that can help you improve your skill at work? Brainstorm by placing those questions in the middle of separate pieces of paper and thinking of everything and anything that fit into those categories. Choose your top ten from the four different categories, place them on your calendar, and schedule at least three times a week to study the given topic.

Now go to the library, Barnes & Noble, Borders, or any other local bookstore and find information on this topic. I take a certain pride in books because you can waste so much time on the Internet searching and getting side-swiped by garbage that attracts your interest. Who hasn't been conned at least once into winning a $500 gift card through clicking away from page to page. Don't lose yourself to the black holes of the Internet. Find a book on the topic. If the first book is bad, that is okay. Move to the next book on the shelf, or ask someone who is an expert in the topic.

Begin the Process Today

Try a new topic every week. What you will find is that you will at some point find a topic you want to continue into another week and that requires more than three times a week to read. Once you have done this, your program is over, and you will continue learning at your own pace. If a topic runs dry after one day of reading, move to a more interesting one. This may lead to a change in your profession or a return to a favorite pastime. It may just make you feel young again. This is why elderly men and women love to take courses at the local community college; they know how important learning is. If you are not learning, your brain is slowly atrophying; and, in a sense, you are dying one day at a time.

I declare the truth and give thanks.
I am perfect as I am in this very moment.
I am beautiful, strong, unconditionally loved, and accepted.
I am _____.
And I am choosing to be happy today.

Thank you for this very breath.
Thank you for allowing me to practice.
Thank you for the abundance of wealth, relationships,
and well-being in the world.
Thank you for _____.

I close my eyes and envision
My dream.
I see myself achieving my goal to become a Renaissance *Man or Woman*
And to _____.
I visualize my newly fulfilled life.

I feel
The gift of this dream and my goal becoming a reality,
The one loving consciousness, which flows through our universe,
Full of unconditional love and acceptance
And this abundance of *(God)* energy.

Celebrate.
Smile.
Have fun
and feel the joy of living.
I give thanks for receiving all of this.
I give thanks for my greater purpose and the overall balance in my life.
And I give thanks for _____.

I declare
My purpose, established by
(God, a higher power, or the universe)
Is to spread unconditional love and acceptance through
_____.

I will constantly be reborn to this moment
without memory or judgment.
I will share all my wealth, relationships, and overall well-being
to improve the quality of life around me.
My *(day, evening, or* _____*.)* will be enjoyable and fulfilling!

Additional Suggested Resources

Csikeszentmihalyi, Mihaly. Flow: *The Psychology of Optimal Experience, Steps Towards Enhancing the Quality of Life.* New York: Harper and Row, 1990.

The Evolving Self: A Psychology for the Third Millennium. New York: Harper Collins, 1993.
> Csikeszentmihalyi teaches about the experience of "flow," which can take place in all different practices. It can be the source, which can drive you to effortless learning. "Flow" is the experience many athletes have when they are in the zone. There is no conscious thinking; many activities can be a source of this happiness.

Glasser, William. *The Quality School: Managing Students Without Coercion.* New York: Harper Collins, 1998.
> This will help you realize how children can learn with less competitive and more group-oriented classrooms. It is one of many of his books that teach you about your own learning as well as your children's. He has a wealth of experience with a diverse group of people, and he shares his ideas in such a humble and non-coercive manner.

Krishnamurti, Jiddu. *The Awakening of Intelligence.* New York: Harper Collins, 1987.

Think of These Things. New York: Harper Collins, 1989.
> Krishnamurti allows you to remove all conditioning in your life to increase the possibility of learning the truth. These books have so much power it is wise to take your time while reading them. They are not books you can read in a weekend; but like religious texts, they draw you into reflection.

Chapter 5

Improving the Quality of Life Around You

Relationships Drive This Pillar

In his movie, Patch Adams proclaims, "If you treat a disease, you win, you lose; but if you treat a person, you'll win… I guarantee you'll win every time". People are what are important; the rest are just distractions. Relationships are what matter the most in life. We are all united; if one is suffering, we all are. As Patch is on trial with the state board of medicine for treating the sick in an unsanctioned clinic, he discusses the issue of transference and the belief that a doctor is taught not to form personal connections with patients. He says that "transference is inevitable"; every person we meet leads to some cause and effect in the interaction. It is up to us to have a positive effect, opening our hearts to all by looking past the labels and appearances to see people for who they are. To improve your quality of life as well as the world's, you must improve your relationships (Williams, 1999).

Most people do not have any relationships in which they are content. Usually, our best friends (the ones you introduce by saying, "I have known her since I was in first grade") are the only healthy relationships we have. These relationships are based on acceptance, and they are priceless. The problem is that we are not involved in enough of these types of relationships.

I always say Aaron and I met on the track during high school, and we have been best friends ever since. Aaron and I are unable to see each other for months and months at a time, but we still are able to jump right into conversations as if we had never been apart when we do see each other. We accept each other. I know that if I haven't heard from him, it is not because he does not care. We don't make false assumptions about the other person.

When you accept someone, you do not take their actions personally, and this allows a friendship to flourish. The only time our friendship wavers is when we break the golden rule of friendship, that is, when one of us is trying to change the other. Although I miss seeing him and wish we lived closer together, I don't blame anyone for this.

As I have previously said, one of the best relationships my wife and I have is with my father because we are accepting of his craziness and he is accepting of our dreams and passions. I have no fear in sharing any ideas because he truly listens to what Ashley and I have to say. We talk for hours in his basement pub, Nardi Inn; but we are unable to have the same relationship with him outside of our safety net. If he comes over to my mother's house or we go over to his house with my siblings, usually he returns to the role of bad father, the label he has been given. The comfort of acceptance is lost. Instantly the roles that we have been able to erase when we are the only ones with him arise when we add any other family member to the mix.

Contrastingly, my mother and I are at the point in our relationship where we have not truly accepted each other. I don't believe anyone is at fault. She has given me everything. No matter when I needed something, she would do everything in her power to help me; yet I have difficulties because of the roles we play. We are blinded by these roles, unable to see the people we are. Slowly we are seeing the truth. We both have flaws, but we are both perfect just the way we are with all our idiosyncrasies, as normal or strange as they may be. I can't wait for the day that we have a relationship again as we did when I was a child because I miss seeing who she truly is.

> Friendship is "one soul inhabiting two bodies."
> —Aristotle

I always plan on visiting and just having fun with her; but her role as mother, my role as son, and the other roles such as in college when I thought I would not want to come back to Cleveland reappear. The whole process is so silly because I allow a million different irrelevant memories to separate us in the present. In these roles, she as a parent tries to help me make the right decisions. All I want her to do is listen to the problems I may have and not try to fix them. I watch many people my same age fight with their parents in this matter. I make assumptions that she feels this way or that, and we become very close but lack any intimacy. We talk on the phone with nothing to say. Why is this?

I believe it is because we have a relationship that is based on our invented roles with no intimacy and, more importantly, no acceptance. I fear sharing who I truly am with her because I feel I might disappoint her. As you will learn, her Catholic faith is strong, and my beliefs vary from hers. I wrote her a letter to tell her all the reasons I loved her and why I am so happy for her. When she called to thank me, I was having a bad day and was unable to be intimate for fear of what might happen. How ridiculously foolish this may seem from your viewpoint because it is. Now I am working to replace any negative thoughts of our relationship with my visualization of us hugging. The law of attraction allows you to bring peace to many relationships, and it is healing this relationship as I write these words.

> *Of all the things which wisdom provides to make life entirely happy, much the greatest is the passion of friendship.*
> —Epicurus

Most people's failed relationships come to an end because they allow roles to get in the way. These roles are so powerful because they are built by the ego. We go to the grocery store, and we classify and place judgment on all who walk past. We label rich, poor, stuck-up, selfish, ugly. Why do we do this? We are not doing it; it is the ego driving us to create a divide. It builds itself up, telling us we are better off than the confused women before us. The ego knows that if it convinces us that we are better than the other person, we will not have the power to change this thinking. The ego gets stronger and stronger. When you become more aware of your ego judging others, stop, take a deep breath, and declare the world is beautiful. Feel love for the person you once judged and smile.

Most relationships are built on fear. We do just enough to keep people in our lives, and we attempt to keep them at any cost to the intimacy of the relationship. We build walls between our family members and coworkers. We create close relationships, which are safe but lack intimacy. This is the cause of so much unhappiness in our lives. We are dying one day at a time, completely alone, because we are afraid to open up. We are afraid of what will happen when people see us for who we really are.

Why are people so afraid? Most have been brainwashed to believe they are ugly, stupid, and weak. They have locked their hearts up, thrown away the key, and emit a negative frequency. The law of attraction ensures these thoughts and roles manifest into broken relationships.

I am sure you have heard the phrase that you are either part of the solution or part of the problem. Based on that, you need to take the responsibility to improve your quality of life and to help others improve theirs. If you're not doing this, you are allowing suffering in your life as well as in the lives of others. This solution may be entering a profession based on helping others, such as doctors, counselors, psychologists, teachers, physical therapists, and nurses, although these are not the only outlets for helping others. Many people in these fields are not improving the quality of life around them because they are unaware of the importance of relationships with their clients. Teachers easily forget the importance of relationship in the rush of daily tasks. Little by little, they may not be driven to improve the quality of their students' lives. As teachers burn out, we see that they are disconnected from their colleagues and students.

Children have always accepted my silly personality. They are not afraid of being who they are if you create an environment, as I have as a counselor and a teacher with them, where there are no roles. They have no time for roles because playing a role is not fun; it is a bad frequency that does not bring in any positive energy. It is fun to just be, and I make them laugh by doing the things we all fear so much. That is just being who I am. I love to play. I am probably one of the oldest kids in the world, and I don't think I will ever stop. I have laughed, joked, cheered, made a fool of myself, danced, sang, and done handstands with the children I have taught. I jump on desks and make the classroom come alive.

Therefore, if relationship is the focus, many careers allow professionals to improve the quality of life around them in their everyday works. They create personal growth and discovery while helping others. As a teacher, I have learned so much. I began with high aspirations, ready to change the world, working in the inner city as a middle school math teacher. I thought I knew so much and that

I would use my charismatic, savvy personality to win the children over. Reflecting upon what I enjoy in the classroom leads to my belief that, in a selfish way, my ego was the founding father of my love of education. When I was an intern in college in psychology, I enjoyed the attention I received as a teacher in a classroom of students with attention hyperactive deficit disorder (ADHD). This is when I transitioned into education, which led me to the greatest challenge of my life.

My Path as an Educator

This experience knocked the wind out of me when I failed to help the adolescent children I thought I could change. At this time, I did not realize how important relationships are in the learning process. Ironically, I tried to quit that first teaching job in the inner city several times; but I had great leaders who would not allow me to leave. They gave me the opportunity to do so but in a way I could not accept. This helped me to realize how ignorant I was. The school had taken a downward slide from bad principals, underpaid teachers, and a declining neighborhood. In the beginning of the school year, I had to speak to over a hundred people, informing them of the new discipline plan that would be in place for their children. They had to think I was crazy.

In addition, I thought pictures of my best friend, who is African American, and his family would gain my students' trust. I was honestly out of my mind. Trust is a hard thing to obtain from anyone, but even more difficult to obtain from people who have lost trust in life and the system that controls their future. Year after year, the teachers who students fall in love with leave them as their fathers and mothers have. For most of the children, school was the only consistency in their lives. When that changed every year, they became fearful of accepting you.

> One can have no smaller or greater mastery than mastery of oneself.
> —Leonardo Da Vinci

I soon realized they did not want to be saved; no one wants that. They wanted to be heard and accepted. I would not allow myself to get close to my students, which I realized was a mistake.

Teachers tell you not to smile before Christmas and don't befriend students or their parents. They are wrong! I learned from my mistakes. Now I know I have to open up to children and see them for the individuals they are. They are drawn to the energy I release into the universe.

The school was in complete disorder. I was continually chastised by parents for disciplining their children for their inappropriate behavior. Then the same parents reprimanded their kids in the middle of the hall for these same actions, using any and every derogatory comment you could think of. Some of the students' mothers threatened the other students. It was apparent this hate was embedded in the thick walls of the building. It finally climaxed with a girl having her shirt and bra ripped entirely off. She was more concerned with losing a shoe than the fact that she running through the halls topless. All the boys were gawking at the situation; it was an utter circus. A priest was thrown to the ground by the other girl in the fight. I gave the topless one my jacket and forced her to cover up as well as move into the restroom away from the disruption I was dealing with in the hallway. The other girl in the brawl had to be contained by the priest who she had caught by surprise and hammered to the floor. The boys just wanted a view of the disrobed girl. I could not believe the pandemonium!

> *Where there is hatred, let me sow love. Where there is injury, pardon. Where there is doubt, faith.*
> *—St. Francis of Assisi*

There are so many different stories I could tell beyond this one, such as the time a boy struck another boy with a Bible. I will not go into any more detail of the confusion because it is more than apparent that there were more fights than actual learning taking place.

Consequently, all that I thought I had learned about teaching was a sham. I awakened very quickly to the fact that I knew absolutely nothing of value that could help me improve this environment and that I had a long voyage ahead of me. Previously, in high school and college, I was overconfident in myself. I was arrogant and thought there was very little I did not know. This teaching position was the most eye-opening experience of my existence. This was the first time I knew only one thing for certain: I knew very little about what the world was really about. What a great lesson! So humbling!

During this second renaissance of my life, I learned to ask for help. This was the first time anyone had done this at the school, and it brought all of us back to the terror of the present moment. As a team of teachers, community members, staff, and administration, we took the school back one day at a time. It was a hard fought battle, but we used force and punishment to do this. This came at the high cost of relationships that I ended and the fear that I instilled. I had to question why I was doing what I was doing. Although these techniques may have prevented further aggression, they did not allow learning to flourish as it would have had the change been based on improving relationships.

Punishment and fear-producing behaviors need to be replaced by love and understanding. Students learn more when they are comfortable and content. They need to know they are loved and that teachers really care about who they are not only as students but as people. This corresponds to all life's relationships in the home, at work, and in the community. You need to realize how beautiful and strong you are. I am here to tell you it is time for your rebirth.

Teaching has enlightened me about how strong my ego once was. I thought I was always right and was more than self-righteous. I ranted about racism and

> *The greatest discovery of my generation is that man can alter his life simply by altering his attitude of mind. As you think, so shall you be.*
> *—William James*

the blatant ignorance of the upper class. I then realized that it is not the upper class, the lower class, the poor, the uneducated, or the professionals who create this lack of awareness. Ego and fear destroy love and compassion; they create hate. Their negative energy emanates into our lives through our thoughts causing the universe to manifest more hate through the law of attraction.

The following year, I moved to a Title I school in Atlanta where yet again the same lack of inspiration from teachers was apparent. They had forgotten how important their relationships with students are. This may have been a direct effect of the principal, who seemed to destroy any relationship she had with the staff by creating an environment of fear. I felt so sorry for her because she seemed to be deprived of any true relationship with any of her employees.

In a time when society is obsessed with achievement tests, relationships in school are lost because they cannot be measured by any paper and pencil assessment. As we allow relationship to diminish, we become emotionally deprived from even ourselves. This is why the great tragedies of our world happen.

There are so many examples in history. As shown by the acceptance of slavery in America, a whole race was taken out of the equation of relationship in our country. Hitler took a whole religious and ethnic group out of the world's relationship during the Holocaust. Murder and rape are committed by people who have no sense of intimacy and relationship in their lives; they are lost in their own world of isolation. When we separate ourselves from mankind, it is inevitable that destruction in our lives will take place.

> *The greater danger for most of us lies not in setting our aim too high and falling short, but in setting our aim too low and achieving our mark.*
> *—Michelangelo*

In Atlanta, I found teaching students who predominantly spoke English as a second language was so much fun and so rewarding because of the intimacy that returned to my heart. I began to create relationships with my students, which gave me more insight into another culture. These students, whose parents were illegal aliens and spoke little or no English, were so family-oriented, and I was blessed to see it. I hope to have the same kind of relationships with my children that those students had with their families.

To teach a child a language is such an amazing experience. I have not had a child of my own yet, but I felt so proud when one of my students who had never spoken English before walking into my classroom could read by the end of the year. Seeing this success stimulated me to study further on the subjects of learning, counseling, and motivating. I went back to receive my masters and became a scholar practitioner.

To motivate and give thanks to such a deprived faculty and student body, two creative minds came together to create a Christmas concert that few will forget. One was a visiting music teacher from

South Africa. The other was a man who successfully produced Grammy-winning performances but became a teacher to give back all he had received. He was a humble man; you never would have known he had accomplished so much. He never spoke of his successes in music unless he was coerced into a discussion. The school gave him the most difficult students, yet never once was he upset or angry. He spoke to the students in an accepting and wise manner, telling his students they could do nothing but succeed. However, on the stage, he was another man entirely. He danced and sang as a James Brown Rudolph, singing with the chorus with such energy. A third grade teacher sang as the Beach Boy Santa, a fifth grade teacher sang the sexy "Santa Baby," and I stumbled through Elvis' "Frosty the Snowman." The children and faculty alike were in shock, smiling, laughing, cheering, and screaming. I had never before performed a day in my life; but for one night, I made the crowd stand on their feet.

These antics continued into crazy hair day and Dr. Seuss's birthday when my long hair stood high and blue. I was Thing 1 and my partner Thing 2, which led to our strange and twisted rendition of Cinderella, in which I had my acting debut as Prince Charming and my counterpart was the first pregnant Cinderella. The play was a going away present that again was an attempt to bring joy into so many broken hearts. I can't say that it was all fun. I fought my way through it with a less than motivated attitude at times, but I can say I was so proud of all us when I saw the children's faces. That may have been the first and last concert or play in their lives. For one day, we brought magic back into their lives. We built strong relationships with each other by giving up any sense of pride and having fun.

After this, I came to a district similar to that of my upbringing, which was a land of overwhelming privilege. The school district had successful test scores. However, this along with the school district's constant change led to a lack of growth in the teachers. This was not because of any lack of caring or work ethic but because the teachers never needed to expand their educational knowledge because of the type of student body they taught. They were always on the top, although they had been battered by administration and parents alike. They were undertrained and overwhelmed by the constant transformation in the direction of the district. The new superintendent had the right ideas, but too much was changed too fast. They were all great people; but as a whole, the district lacked that spark that creates an environment of excellence.

Motivation is fundamental. It is why teachers empower students to accomplish their dreams and rise above soaring teacher expectations. All three schools I taught in had teachers who were awesome and brought the classrooms and hallways to life every moment of the day. I have learned so much from these teachers and my students.

I have been more than lucky to have had the experiences I encountered. People don't realize how wonderful their situations are unless they have previously had worse circumstances. The confidence I gained from my prior teaching experiences diminished in this new position because of my attempting to fill a need of an established group of teachers who didn't desire any help. I had two job descriptions, one of which was to help students, who were struggling with reading and math; for the other, I was asked to help the teachers transition to differentiated instruction. This is teaching each student at their developmental level, having multiple groups in the same class, as opposed to teaching to only one ability level as most textbooks do. This was a very difficult transition for the teachers. They were tired of changes; they were putting their feet down, and I did not realize what an error I had made. I should have begun the process worrying not about strategies but about the people who were in the classrooms. I should have accepted them for all they had done and for all the great things they had accomplished. I thought I could help, but I realized that we saw two different problems. If I had built the relationships first, I might have helped more. Therefore, when the opportunity arose, I chose to go back to a regular third grade classroom instead of my new found role.

This all transpired after I had applied for another job in the same school district, but I was not chosen for the job. The more deserving candidate allowed me to take his teaching position after he was given the position we both applied for. The district wanted me to stay in my current position, but I really felt my passion for teaching vanishing. So, I fought to teach in third grade. I had been overwhelmed by not being accepted or respected for my past experience and the knowledge acquired through those experiences in difficult environments and gained in my master's program by the other teachers in the district.

What I did not realize was that it had nothing to do with all this ego-driven thinking; it was an awakening that I was not meant to be a teacher. I thought that my opinion or knowledge was more effective than the other teachers' practices and that I should be treated better. Although these two beliefs may or may not have been the truth, in reality, the real problem was that I did not want to teach anymore. After breaking down in front of the administrators as a result of these egoic thought patterns as I previously mentioned, I awakened to the fact that I needed to make a change in my life.

> *Human it is to have compassion on the unhappy.*
> —*Giovanni Boccaccio*

The embarrassment of crying in the presence of these administrators makes me laugh now. I was so lost at this point, obviously to the extent that I completely lost control of my emotions. This is another example of how identifying with the ego leads to so much pain and suffering. I was reborn to my new purpose— writing. It did not manifest until months later, but it originated out of this experience.

I transitioned into a new position, and I began to identify with my pure consciousness. In the classroom, I have slowly built new relationships. This experience has taught me to love and respect all people no matter where their paths have taken them. I began writing this book, and the rest is history.

My rebirth allowed me to realize I now will educate through writing and speaking, but I am thankful for the time I have had in this profession. These experiences have led to many insights. In some sense, education has given me an overabundance of opportunity to improve the quality of the world around me, although now I realize through these writings that there is more that I can bring to the table. My dream is getting bigger. As you practice these pillars, your dreams will exponentially grow larger than you ever thought possible.

Self-growth is inevitable if you go into a profession to help others. It has not been a storybook and I have lost my direction along the way, but my focus has allowed me to keep moving in the right direction. When people ask me why I would leave education, I feel liberated from past thinking patterns. I am aware that my path is beyond the limited view I previously had.

There are many accessible ways for all people to achieve this pillar. Although teaching has been my path, I would not suggest it be yours. You have to find your own path to achieve this pillar, but you can achieve this without changing your profession.

Viktor Frankl, as explained earlier, accounts attitude as his means of survival in the Nazi death camps. He shaped a theory that any person can survive any situation because the last choice in life that can never be taken away is your attitude. This attitude can be formed by any drive you may have found, such as your spouse, work, religion, or whatever you see fit. Whatever inspires you to rise above adversity can be used in applying this logotherapy to ensure meaning in your life (1984).

If you are lucky enough to be driven by this purpose to have a profession that allows you to improve the quality of life around you directly, be thankful. However, if you are like most people in the world who work for the sole purpose of paying the bills, you can practice this pillar by building relationships through your words and actions The way people use their words and actions can effect great change around them; words are the direct cause of creating or eliminating relationships.

The five practices that improve the quality of life are listening with unconditional love, acceptance, ending negativity, continuously complimenting others, and positive action. These are the tools that bring an abundance of love and acceptance into your life and the world around you.

The Five Scaffolds of This Pillar

Listening With Your Entire Body

True relationship is based on unconditional love. This is a love built on acceptance and allows you to listen without memory. Most of us fail to listen because we relate everything to ourselves. Instead, we need to listen with our whole bodies. Listen by asking questions, giving eye contact, and acknowledging what the speaker is truly saying. All of us want to feel that people will take the time to love us just for who we are and not for who others want us to be. Through teaching, I have learned how to listen to parents and accept their concerns. They are then more capable of reciprocating the acceptance of my ideas and what is best for their child.

Listening allows us not to be trapped in the roles that define us in our family and work. We can be the savior, the failure, the leader, the listener, and many other roles. Once a role is placed on us, we lose any idea of intimacy with our family. Listening and unconditional love create good relationships and improve the quality of life around us by overcoming these roles.

Listening is such an absent ability in the modern era. With television and so many apathetic opportunities for entertainment in the world today, conversation is a lost love; it is not respected. Usually people talk at you and not to you because most people feel they are not heard. Their egos take over their thoughts and lead them to rant about this and that. It is time we begin to listen to our friends and counterparts alike. Unconditional love and, more importantly, acceptance enable friendship to grow and reduce ego-driven hate. I find that when someone is talking, if I focus on my breathing, it helps to settle my mind to listen to the speaker. I also make eye contact.

Many times, I see first hand that students do not listen to each other and that they are waiting to be heard.

> *Courage is what it takes to stand up and speak; courage is also what it takes to sit down and listen.*
> *—Winston Churchill*

They are always waiting for their turn, struggling to hear their peers. We work on listening in school. I have some rules to help my students listen. They may not raise their hands while another is speaking. They have to focus their attention on the speaker as well. We practice summarizing and asking questions about what the speaker has said. Asking questions and giving eye contact are immediate reinforcements to the speaker that you are listening. The acceptance speakers feel heals their hearts and souls. It teaches them to listen to others. This acceptance and willingness to listen to others will spread through the world as this skill is cultivated.

Giving Respect to All Through Acceptance

Accepting the individuals you meet and giving them respect are ways to begin this scaffold. Relationship is built on mutual respect and acceptance. This begins with saying hello to everyone you see walking on the streets, in your profession, or in the community, especially when they appear to be frustrated or angry. It does not matter if they are black, white, purple, Catholic, Jewish, Islamic, Chinese, American, Russian, women, men, adults, children, young, or old because we are all one. We are only divided by our egos. There is no other disconnect.

For it is in giving that we receive; It is in pardoning that we are pardoned; It is in dying to self that we are born to eternal life.
—St. Francis of Assisi

The human body is built the same; there are minor differences our minds contort into major distinctions. Self-fulfilling prophecy is inevitable; most believe the worst in people and that is what they see. If they give people a chance before ridding themselves of them, people will surprise them.

Hate can't be beaten out of the world. No unified army can do this. Love, optimism, and attitude are learned traits. They are not natural, and most humans learn best from example. Martin Luther King, Jr. and Gandhi shocked the world by not fighting back with their fists or their minds because they knew there was only one thing that could overcome all odds—love. It is too powerful to deny and too strong to be overcome by the ego.

Therefore, always greet your neighbor with a smile, stop judging, and start loving. You will change the world one smile at a time. See every new face on the street as an opportunity to learn something new. Ask people questions and learn their stories. Learn about their dreams and aspirations, help them to find peace in their lives, and fill their empty hearts.

Ending Negative Thoughts, Habits, and Actions

You need to become aware that any negativity hurts you more than the one to whom you are imparting it. As you see that we are part of the same field of energy and you become aware of the law of attraction manifesting what is in your mind into reality, the more negativity you think about and draw towards others, the more negativity will find its way back into your life. This will be more easily seen after you read about the one universal mind, body, and spirit. However, you need to become aware of this idea as you read this scaffold for improving the quality of life.

Using gratitude and visualization, you can easily achieve success in this scaffold. Both can be used at any time your mind is retaking your consciousness. Being thankful for all you have and not being in any way jealous of others helps you maintain your self-worth. Anytime you feel negativity approaching, return to the celebration of life.

> *When angry, count to ten before you speak. If very angry, a hundred.*
> *—Thomas Jefferson*

Give thanks for what you have and feel nothing but love for others. Think of positive dreams and aspirations. The law of attraction will allow the universe to end incessant thinking. Negativity stands no chance against positive thoughts and affirmations.

Negative speech is the ego's most powerful weapon. We need to take it at face value because it can dismantle any relationship you have. If you think negatively, the universe brings you more. The ego is deep-seated; the only way to control it is by strengthening your sense of self-love, which is hard to do in a world that promotes incompetence and leisure time as goals instead of quality and the work ethic. We are brainwashed to believe we need more stuff and more time to relax and enjoy life. We work and we work some more, always working towards more stuff. By the end, we've missed our lives. We've missed our children's first baseball games, our anniversaries, and simple conversations.

> *What do you despise? By this you are truly known.*
> *—Michelangelo*

Most people only realize this when they encounter a near-death situation. It is the small things that count, the moments that can't be romanticized in a movie or book that make our lives full. It is going to work late so you can spend some extra time with your wife or husband; it's turning off your cell phone or Blackberry to listen to a child passionately speak about something they have learned.

This brings us back to what we do not want to do and that is shed responsibility for our actions. A wise man said, "All we have is our word." If this is true, we do not want to tell inaccurate stories. Gossiping is the woman's vice; it only builds the ego more and more while diminishing intimacy. Men usually boast more than women, driven by their arrogance, which is formed by their egos. However, negativity sees no gender; either of the two practices can overtake you.

Every time you take from another by speaking falsely about that person you build the ego and hatred in yourself. There is an age-old rule in teaching when it is time for parent conferences: For every negative, you must say three positives. Always start a conference with a positive; it is human nature to become defensive when people speak negatively about you or your child. Effective teachers know this, and we hope they apply it in the rest of their lives.

> *Do as we say and not as we do.*
> *—Giovanni Boccaccio*

In any good relationship, there is very little blaming or complaining; otherwise, it wouldn't be a good relationship. Most people have a favorite family member or mentor with whom they use positive talk; enlightened people use it with all people. Think of that aunt, uncle, or cousin who was really interested in you and took the time to listen, or it may have been a friend or a mentor. What they all have in common is acceptance. They do not criticize you; they do not offer advice unless asked to do so. There is so much pain in families because of the negative thoughts, habits, and actions we use against each other, which is why so much tension is formed in homes.

Additionally, body language can cause pain in others. How many times have we stared down or made gestures at someone who has cut us off on the road. We spread their misery into our minds by reacting to this ignorance. Has it ever made you arrive at your destination any earlier or made your day go better? Those are the actions that cause us to depress. Reactions are common in incessant thinkers because they have no control over their negativity. In a positive light, how good do you feel when someone waves you in when you are running late? Spread the abundance of love around the world instead of buying into negativity. Use the law of attraction to draw in everything you want in life.

Spreading Your Happiness Through Compliments

Compliments are infectious. They are a way to spread our love and enhance our relationships. When I say they are infectious, I am not saying they are infectious for the receiver but for the giver: Once you start giving them, you can't stop. You are giving out your love, and it multiplies in your heart exponentially. The more you give, the more you realize that we are all one. This increases your self-love. You begin to see the beauty apparent in all things. It is almost a giddy sensation. You feel overwhelmed, and you want everyone to feel it. You are sincere in your word, which makes others feel your love. However, a compliment is only as good as the person who gives it.

> *I am very little inclined on any occasion to say anything unless I hope to produce some good by it.*
> *—Abraham Lincoln*

If you want to give a compliment with lasting effect, as Tom Raft and Donald O. Clifton explain in their book *How Full Is Your Bucket*, the compliment needs to be "individualized, specific, and deserved" (2004, p.80). You cannot give random compliments to anyone and think this will improve the quality of life around you. When you see someone do a specific action that you sincerely feel is of great importance, think of a manner in which you can compliment the individual.

As a teacher, I see children wave off many compliments because they know they did not create quality work. When a compliment is given for an action that is not considered of any consequence, it is wasted breath. Contrastingly, when students feel they have completed quality work, are singled out for this, and given meaningful praise, the students look as if they are floating, feeling the compassion and love throughout their bodies.

Accepting compliments is more difficult than giving them. When you give them, you are better able to receive. Giving compliments ends competition and separation because you see yourself in another. You spread acceptance throughout the world with gratitude. Your heart overflows; your inner body radiates this frequency, which is transmitting unconditional love to all. When you are positive, your quality of life improves and natural endorphins are released.

Taking Positive Action to Effect Change in the World

Finally, the last scaffold is to take action to help others in need. This may be as simple as bringing chicken noodle soup to a sick friend or delivering clothing to a homeless shelter.

As a child, I encountered many experiences helping others through the social concerns group at my church. I met wonderful people who have helped so many. We had a core group of people who raised me who met every weekend to sell donuts before and after all the masses on Sundays, among many other charitable activities. We went downtown once a month to prepare and serve a meal at a soup kitchen. There were countless trips when we delivered

> *From a little spark may burst a flame.*
> *—Dante Alighieri*

bakery goods. I remember being greeted by "Big Hands" on most Sundays during my adolescence. I never knew his name, but he always welcomed us with an enormous smile, which brought endless amounts of joy to all our hearts. His one hand devoured yours as he shook it, and with his other hand, he would magically grab the trays. He had a rough life, but he never made one complaint in all the years I knew him. He was just one of the people who spread love in an area filled with confusion.

My mother has based her life on helping others. She has caused many others to do the same. Think of how many people you can help. Through your example, you can affect exponential numbers if they affect others through your example. If you haven't noticed, I often quote from movies. One that is a great example of this scaffold is Pay It Forward. A teacher trying to inspire students to change the world creates a spark in one boy, who invents the concept of "paying it forward." If you can help three people in an unexpected and unconditional manner in a way that cannot be repaid, ask them to pay it forward. If they help three people who help three people who help three more people, you have indirectly helped eighty-one people. This can keep growing exponentially (That's the idea, 2001).

Improving the quality of life can take place in many forms. I have only grazed the surface of all the ways you can improve the quality of life around you. Give all you have because there is abundance in your life, which is overflowing. Give and you will receive even more abundance. Contrastingly, if you believe you are sacrificing, you will send out negative transmissions; and your life won't be as full. Realize there is no end to the amount of love in this world. Love runs rampant throughout the universe; it draws from an infinite source.

Further Study Into Improving the Quality of Life

Don Miguel Ruiz has written many beautiful, spiritual books. If you are looking to learn more about how to practice the five scaffolds of this pillar, he has written three books that are guides to these practices. They have an overall theme of acceptance of yourself, others, and relationship. *The Mastery of Love: A Practical Guide to the Art of Relationship* is a wonderful book to work on the relationships in your life, which can become a source of strength. Like Glasser's *Choice Theory: A New Psychology of Personal Freedom*, it allows the reader to realize that most pain and suffering in the present is caused not by an outside force, such as your spouse or parents, but by the way you choose to behave in

> *The secret of getting things done is to act.*
> *—Dante Alighieri*

your relationships (1998). You can control your mind and actions in a way that allows you to be unaffected by other's unconscious acts.

Ruiz's book *The Four Agreements: A Practical Guide to Personal Freedom* is based on overcoming our domestication of past agreements and building new agreements, which allow you to live a fulfilled life. It is another approach to this pillar if you have not gained enough grounding from my writing. It will allow you to take power over your life and hold yourself more responsible in the way you contribute to society. When you realize other people's actions are not meant to harm you but are directly caused by their unawareness (the universal ego), you can use your words and actions to improve the quality of life around you. By not making assumptions and being wounded by others' words and actions, you can manage your life more easily (1997). My relationships have diminished at times because of the assumptions I have made about family members, colleagues, my wife, and many others. Don't allow this separation, which I have allowed, to reduce these relationships that are so important in your life. Accept yourself, which allows you to accept others and to become intimate with all the people in your life.

On a final note, you have a homework assignment to watch the movie Patch Adams, which tells his story of how he evolved into the man he is today. He was driven to overcome his depression in the pursuit of helping others. This is one of Robyn Williams's most moving roles. He will teach you how to build relationships, and we see how his Gesundheit Institute was created. Overcoming his depression through helping those around him, he is a great example of the law of attraction. He is thankful for every moment, and he gives without sacrifice. He knows of the abundance this world has stockpiled, and he draws upon it every day of his life. He has inspired me and he can inspire you!

I declare the truth and give thanks.
I am perfect as I am in this very moment.
I am beautiful, strong, unconditionally loved, and accepted.
I am _____.
And I am choosing to be happy today.

Thank you for this very breath.
Thank you for allowing me to practice.
Thank you for the abundance of wealth, relationships,
and well-being in the world.
Thank you for _____.

I close my eyes and envision
My dream.
I see myself achieving my goal to become a Renaissance *Man or Woman*
And to _____.
I visualize my newly fulfilled life.

I feel
The gift of this dream and my goal becoming a reality,
The one loving consciousness, which flows through our universe,
Full of unconditional love and acceptance
And this abundance of *(God)* energy.

Celebrate.
Smile.
Have fun
and feel the joy of living.
I give thanks for receiving all of this.
I give thanks for my greater purpose and the overall balance in my life.
And I give thanks for _____.

I declare
My purpose, established by
(God, a higher power, or the universe)
Is to spread unconditional love and acceptance through
_____.

I will constantly be reborn to this moment
without memory or judgment.
I will share all my wealth, relationships, and overall well-being
to improve the quality of life around me.
My *(day, evening, or* _____.*)* will be enjoyable and fulfilling!

Additional Suggested Resources

Choice Theory: A New Psychology of Personal Freedom. New York: Harper Collins, 1998.
> Choice theory has the power to make you more accountable for the happiness in your life. You will stop being a victim, and you will regain control over your life. This is a very analytical book, which will help logical thinkers break through to solve their problems.

Glasser, William & Glasser, Caroline. *Getting Together and Staying Together.* New York: Harper Collins, 2000.
> *Getting Together and Staying Together* is a wonderful book to read individually or with your significant other to find your essential needs. This will help you to see what forms of love you like to receive, and it will enable you to understand how to love without judgment. You will awaken to your quality worlds, and this will help you to establish relationships that will last. Glasser has multiple books in addition to the ones mentioned to help you with your children at school as well as during their teenaged years through their teaching of choice theory.

Malone, Thomas. & Malone Patrick. *The Art of Intimacy.* New York: Prentice Hall, 1987.
> This book goes in depth into the idea of the ego, closeness, and intimacy. It has helped my wife and I find contentment and acceptance in each other. You will be able to see your friends and family for the wonderful people they are without judgment.

Napier, Augustus. & Whitaker, Carl. *The Family Crucible: The Intense Experience of Family Therapy.* New York: Perennial Library, 1978.
> They have helped so many in ending inaccurate roles, which have bound too many family relationships. I have utilized their teachings to improve the quality of my relationships without role identification. It is helpful to see real life examples of families to relate to.

Rath, Thomas. & Clifton, Donald. *How Full Is Your Bucket? Positive Strategies of Work and Life.* New York: Gallup Press, 2004.
These two psychologists have researched the power of positive thought and action in life. It is an awesome book to raise your awareness and excitement of the power of a positive balance in your life. It is a quick read, which I use when I find myself being overtaken by the mind. It will teach the power of a compliment, among other techniques, to maintain positive thought patterns.

Ruiz, Miguel. *The Four Agreements: A Practical Guide to Personal Freedom.* San Rafael, CA: Amber Allen Publishing, 1997.

The Mastery of Love: A Practical Guide to the Art of Relationship. San Rafael, CA: Amber Allen Publishing, 1999.

The Voice of Knowledge: A Practical Guide to Inner Peace. San Rafael, CA: Amber Allen Publishing, 2004.
Miguel is a Toltec teacher, which means he teaches through the many great prophets of the world in an eclectic approach to allow you to forgive, stop being a victim, find true happiness in yourself, and share your love with others. He will teach the idea of the story teller. This will enable you to see the truth and falseness of every voice you hear.

The Dalai Lama. *An Open Heart: Practicing Compassion in Everyday Life.* New York: Little Brown and Company, 2001.
His Holiness writes about life and meditation to improve the quality of all our lives through compassion and a cessation of suffering. He has won the Nobel Peace Prize for good reason. His wisdom of the Buddha and compassion will empower you to spread this love to all sentient beings.

Chapter 6

Spirituality: Pursuit of the Truth

Reverencing Life

Spirituality is a word with multiple meanings; its meaning really depends on who you are asking. Therefore, I will define it in the context of this text: It is reverencing all that is. It is identifying with pure consciousness in this moment and erasing any identification with the lie or the ego's incessant thinking. In the past, I explained it in another manner; but with help of Domenico, I have realized its different appearances. He asked me if I thought he was a spiritual man, and I wavered at this question. He was not a practicing anything, and he always questioned my beliefs. So how could he possibly be spiritual? When I turned the question back to him, he firmly believed he was.

Domenico helped me realize that no institution is spiritual in itself. A church is created by form, which directly separates it from the one universal consciousness, although through the people who are conscious of what is, there is spirituality in most religions. Most religions relate to the idea of the imperfection of man. Through their teachings of sin and suffering, they promote the idea of the lie. Man is not flawed; he is not the cause of sin and suffering. The ego is the external cause of all of this, and in western reli-

> *Great men are they who see that the spiritual is stronger than the material force, that thoughts rule the world.*
> *—Ralph Waldo Emerson*

gions there is also an external belief in God causing this confusion. Furthermore, we are God; however, we are not the lie. We are all connected to this pure consciousness, and all the power of this world is in us. Even though people believe in the external God, they still are with him in his presence; and this is where spirituality arises in modern religions. If these same people enlightened themselves to the

111

truth of reality, they would evolve to a higher level of spirituality and would be reborn; but they are currently limited by these beliefs.

Renaissance Men or Women practice spirituality in every breath they take. They are engaged in everything they do, and they easily access this higher power. Spirituality can take place in a church, at work, at home, or in nature. My spirituality was reborn not in any church but through what I found to be the two most unlikely practices. Meditation and yoga have allowed me to be present in this moment and have taught me to enjoy every moment of life with the breath as my guide. As I walk through the forest during my sacred runs, I see the utter beauty of this world through every leaf, flower, and tree.

You may or may not be a practicing Catholic, Christian, Buddhist, Muslim, or Hindu. Your religion is irrelevant to spirituality unless you find presence through it. Even though I currently attend a Lutheran church, I do not affiliate myself with this religion or my Catholic upbringing. I do recognize the truth in both of these different sects, which is the words Jesus used to teach us the concept of heaven on earth. His teachings awaken me to the fact that, as I drink tea and I feel the warmth flow into my mouth and down my throat, I am in the present.

I am practicing this pillar as I write the words on this page. As I reverence every breath I take, I celebrate the spirit of God. This can be defined as positive energy, love, and many other names; but what they all have in common is the feeling of their presence in your mind, body, and spirit.

All of us take our own paths, and I will not judge or recommend one to you. I will show you what yours may or may not look like by sharing the story of my greatest teacher. I will also share my forever changing path from my childhood until this present moment, which has not been as sound as my mother's.

An Evolution of Spirituality

My mother finds spirituality in her faith. She has been a dedicated Catholic since the day she was born. I have yet to meet someone as strong in unwavering faith. This has enabled her to overcome so much pain in her lifetime. She has shared her faith with all of us. She is the perfect example of someone who finds their spirituality in an institutional religion, but we can evolve into a more elevated sense of spirituality. We can move away from the lie that we have a flawed humanity and draw from the overabundant source of love when you are reborn to the realization that God is from within. He is not outside of us.

As a child, I went to church with her. Our priest would ask me to retell the readings and their meaning. I remember the warmth of the stories, the certainty, and the security they gave me. Then one day it all ended; I can't tell you when or for what reason, but I realized the stories I had retold did not equate to the reality we live in. The rules that I learned were not as sound as I had first anticipated; the people, the church, and the world were not as simple as the Bible appeared to portray all of them to be. As a result, when I lost my innocence, my spirituality suffered. All I carried from my faith was the belief that I was a sinner and that I needed to repent for my sins. I stopped loving God and myself, and I lost any sense of spirituality. I have been trying to regain it since I became aware that it was gone.

> **The Proven Power of Spirituality**
> *Spirituality highly correlates with decreased anger, an increased resilience in the face of day-to-day problems, and an overall improved quality of life.*
> Kennedy et al, 2002

I have become conscious of the fact that there is no perfect religion. After rejecting my own in the hope of finding the right path, I have found that the truth is the only thing that matters. Great spiritual teachers, gods, prophets, or whatever you may call them have surprisingly the same message. From Jesus to Buddha, there is this awareness that suffering or sin is in the world, caused by ignorance and separation from God and your soul. But what they do not teach is that this suffering and sin are not of our making, they are external. The ego and its incessant thinking are the cause of all suffering. However, these great spiritual leaders also teach the law of attraction and explain that there is an abundance of love you can share with all. So, if you can become aware of this abundance inside your heart, which can attract more love into your life, and forget about the idea that you are a sinner or a cause of suffering, you will become a Renaissance Man who is spiritual.

My mother had faith that was as solid as a rock. I never heard her speak a false word about God. He has given her purpose to achieve all she has set out to do. At times when her life is in confusion, her faith gives her grounding. She is a servant of God and strives to help all in need. She uses Jesus as her model to help all who need it. She shares her beliefs and faith with all she encounters, without force or a false sense of pride. This allows her to spoil anyone with whom she comes in contact, starting with our family and continuing to the inner city. She gives thanks for all she has and shares all her love with abundance. It has given her wisdom, which has enlightened her to understand that this abundance is without end. She draws upon whatever is needed and gives it to all. When she is lost, she prays and reads the Bible. This has empowered her to overcome so many challenges in her life, which few would ever be able to bear.

> **The Proven Power of Spirituality**
> *There is nearly a 70% chance patients with AIDs will increase their spirituality/religion. Over 30% say their lives are now better than before being diagnosed with AIDs because of their newly acquired spirituality.*
>
> Szaflarski et al, 2006

Therefore, the unwavering faith of my mother has great strength, but I believe there is exponential possibility in all of us when we move past faith and come to see the truth. We are all perfect in every breath we take. Furthermore, there are three reasons spirituality is important. First is the sense of community it forms. Second is the security it provides in times of loneliness. Third is the humbling, as well as the calming, that there is more than what is seen in the world. People need to understand these truths when all else has forsaken them. All the different forms enable all walks of life to find these essential understandings and reverence this perfect moment that is now.

The Universe Is One Body, Mind, and Soul

The one undivided and most important idea that allows us to break away from our self-absorbed neurotic lives is that we share the same common fears, thoughts, and worries. It is a collective unconscious that we all have that is created by the mind's incessant thinking. Some have called it original sin or ignorance; but no matter what you call it, all the different ideas are formed from the same accord. They are all a lie created by the mind to separate us from who we truly are. Therefore, past religious thought is limiting. We need to go past it and think not of the weakness of humanity but of the abundance and possibility. We are not flawed; we are not sinners. We are one. The ego is the flaw, but we are not this. We are pure consciousness.

We are branches of the same tree, all interconnected. We need to stop thinking of the external

> *When I investigate and when I discover the forces of the heavens and planets are within ourselves, then truly I seem to be living among the gods.*
> —*Leon Battista Alberti*

power that is supposedly "all knowing" and has control of our lives. The human belief that we are powerless is debilitating in every sense of the word. Doubt leaches on to this lie and creates division in the world. We think that we are incomplete, so we are incomplete. The law of attraction can't be broken, and this is why this lie still lives today. If you are not perfect in your mind and you think constantly of these imperfections in your life, they spread like cancer throughout your body.

Prayer can be a realization of the strength in us. It is a practice that should not lead to a feeling of powerlessness. Self-fulfilling prophecy is apparent every day in my life. I know I will make the choices that need to be made to improve the quality of my life, and I find peace in the truth that this power is in all of us.

"God" is another word to describe that which is indescribable; however, the concept connotes the idea of something external. There is no entity beyond our flesh; the universe is made of the same contents. If there is a God, he is in all of us. There is no chemical or matter that we do not all share. This very fact should lead you to accept that all is beautiful. Your enemy is God, you are God, and the ocean is God.

If we see that these thoughts that run continually through our minds minute after minute, day after day, and year after year are all the same, we will begin to accept them for what they are, just thoughts. We need to step back and realize they are not who we are. We need to help each other rid our souls of this discontent. Our minds are so similar; yet through the ideas of race, religion, and borders, we are constantly dividing ourselves. Stop! It is not worth the energy that you are expending to see differences in your spouse, siblings, parents, friends, and enemies. We are no different; the same hate that floods all our minds is apparent in every individual we meet. More importantly, there is something more powerful in all of us. Love, God, positive energy, or whatever you may call it is abundantly flowing through the universe.

This is a very powerful understanding that Jesus taught: "Love your neighbor as yourself" (Mark 12:29-31 NIJ). Once you realize this, you will see how spreading our suffering affects us. The love we found when we first saw our wives, husbands, or children is no different than any other pure love. Spirituality and a belief in a higher power allow us to share this feeling with all. It breaks down borders, opens walls, and divides conflict by ending turmoil, which evolves into peace. Once you see this one truth that is so apparent in the world, you will let down your guard and accept yourself, your wife or husband, and your mother as well as your father. You will start every day anew with no residue of the past, pain, or suffering. You will spread your love instead of your fear and hate. You will smile, laugh, and cry more. Overcome the ego and you will be reunited with this love, which is God, pure consciousness, and a higher power.

Man is what he believes.
—Anton Chekhov

The verdict is out; we finally know. What do we know? We cannot have one without the other because at their core both science and religion lead to the same truth: one universal body, mind, and spirit. How have religion and science proved this? Modern science has found that nothing is material, from the smallest particle on this earth and in the universe. There is more space than anything. The vast space we speak of as "stillness" is in every atom of our bodies; we are walking and talking protons and neutrons. You are not a physical being; you are a moving force.

> *Science without religion is lame; religion without science is blind.*
> —*Albert Einstein*

Basically, when you break it down in simple terms, your body is made up of space and moving charges. There is nothing physical about you, and there is nothing that makes you different from anyone else because we are all this constant flow of energy. The body is continually replacing its cells at such a rapid rate that within a week, month, or year there is no way you have the same body with which you began.

This awareness of the rebirth of the body should allow us to have a mental rebirth. This is why we should be constantly reborn to the present moment. This proves it; now we really know. The world is nothing but a force of motion, which is mostly filled with space.

All the religious teachers since Buddha, Moses, and Jesus have talked of this idea of God, a spirit, or a universal higher power to which we are all connected. Their followers may argue the details, but the teachings all have the same main idea: We are here to stay. Like our regenerative cells, we may transfer our energy into new cells, but we are here nonetheless. Every time your body reproduces itself, you are still the same awareness before you took this new body. This awareness has been apparent since the beginning of time. Don't think you are anything more than anyone else. This is why your judgments, sins, ignorance, and any negative actions always come back to you. When you act against someone, you are really picking a fight against yourself. This awareness will help you to forgive as I did, and it will enhance your life.

We are all one body, spirit, and mind, which is God or whatever you may call it. Love unconditionally with complete acceptance and give thanks that science and religion have finally kissed and made up. Never be fooled by either one of their illusions; see the truth they both can offer. Whenever you give this unconditional love into the universe, the law of attraction reciprocates an abundance of this energy back to you. As you start this process, you miraculously feel this continuous energy return to you without end.

In conclusion, you can flow like water down the stream, loving all there is; or you can fight against the stream. Fighting against the current will create division in your life, manifesting in borders, disparity, and negativity. This will turn into poor relationships, although you could just float along in bliss. To cultivate this energy, utilize the awareness of the abundance in the world and draw upon it. Once you do this, you will see every new face as a member of the immediate family you have been waiting to meet. While looking at your enemies, you will realize they are part of your larger family to whom you have to make amends to feel complete again. This will give you pleasure beyond your imagining.

The Anchors of Prayer and Meditation

Meditation has become a sacred place of prayer for me in my life. Although all I am doing is inhaling and exhaling, I feel I have a place of refuge. The world can be lonely even when the house is full of people, but spirituality and an awareness in a higher power allow you to find peace in times of great pain and suffering.

In the Buddhist tradition, the goal of life is to relinquish the ego. As you establish the practice, this is exactly what happens. You stop trying to be and start accepting who you are. The past and the future collide into the present moment where you become aware of the interconnected universe from a butterfly flying in the park all the way out into space to every shooting star. Sitting when you are bored enlightens you to the fact that you are not as alone as you feel. You discover what I previously discussed, that we see the world through similar eyes. You witness firsthand that we are all one and one in all.

> The soul contains the event that shall befall it, for the event is only the actualization of its thoughts, and what we pray to ourselves for is always granted.
> —Ralph Waldo Emerson

This awakening or rebirth can appear through many experiences. Some people find it in their artwork, writing, or even in the practice of reading. This is simply being with yourself and the whole world at the same time without saying a word. It is a moment you can visualize your new life and feel the warmth and affection it brings to your heart. During these experiences, give thanks for what you have and your new life, which is right here in this very moment. Use the law of attraction to bring peace to your mind, replacing any sorrow and pain with an abundance of positive energy.

There are many examples of specific prayers and meditations that can be of great use to you. You are continually practicing one of them as you finish each chapter. I have found two great examples that have helped me overcome hard times. The first is *The Prayer of Jabez: Breaking Through to the Blessed Life*, which is a book written by Bruce Wilkinson and a prayer from the Bible. This prayer allows you to ask without fear because of your awareness of this abundance that has been spoken of. God is waiting to share it with you. All you have to do is ask, which is just another analogy for self-fulfilling prophecy and the law of attraction. This prayer allows you to create your dreams (2000).

The second example is the meditation of love and kindness. Any Buddhist book will have a different form of it. All you have to do is bring awareness of unconditional love and compassion for yourself. Then you can extend it to your friends and family, a stranger, your enemy, and all sentient beings. The feeling is essential in this meditation; the warmth and acceptance for yourself will allow you to focus upon specific individuals, bringing kindness into their hearts by drawing from the abundance of energy the world holds.

> **The Proven Power of Prayer and Meditation**
> *Stress and other symptoms can be reduced by using silent mantram (prayers) repeated in a spiritual manner as a means to improve the quality of life for patients as well as nurses.*
> Bormann et al, 2005

Community Builds Love and Belonging

Community, which is such an intricate part of love and belonging, is one of our essential needs in life. This connects us to the universal consciousness and the awareness that we are not separate. When I was a child, my mother with the help of a priest and a wonderfully dedicated group of people created the Social Concerns Committee at our church. It made church more interesting when you had others to share the experience with. We were always the first to arrive and the last to leave. We were either packing the car, selling donuts, or carrying boxes. We sold donuts every week to raise money, and we also took the monthly trips to the hunger center to cook and serve meals. Finally, we delivered pastries, left over food, baskets, and presents. It wasn't always fun. As a child, I complained more than you could imagine.

What made it easier as I grew older was my friends beginning to come along to help.

You don't have to be Catholic or even religious to find a reason to gather with a group of friends to help those in need. You can visit the hunger center once a month or work the window at an inner city church, handing out donuts and coffee. Deliver some food with a close friend to a sick friend who is need of some company. Hold the door open for a person who is clearly searching for a helping hand. On the other hand, if you want to find a sense of community in your church and you are still waiting for a seat for Christmas Mass, find another place to fulfill this need.

Unfortunately, church seems to be the one place that one minute you are shaking people's hands for the sign of peace and fifteen minutes later they are cutting in front of you rushing out of the parking lot. Why is everyone rushing? Where do they need to go? Why did they even come to church? Are they running away from God? I can't answer any of those questions. The sense of community has been taken from both our neighborhoods and churches. Church seems to be a place where people can't arrive on time but are always ready to leave before it ends. Now I know that I haven't given churches a fair view here. Church is still a wonderful place. I just miss the community feel it once had.

Nevertheless, I have enjoyed the new sense of community at my wife's church. I feel as I did as a child. It might be because the church is out in the country, or it might just be the simple fact that the greeter is a friend of my wife's family and he gives me a hand shake, a smile, and a hug. When you are greeted like this, there is no chance of doing anything but enjoying the service. This is how I remember my childhood. It is not a place where everyone claims to be saved or judges your faith the way some small churches I have encountered do. The congregants are accepting and loving with no conditions attached. Everyone just seems content. You can see it in their calm faces. The pastor greets all visitors, welcoming them to the church, celebration, and communion. The singing is inspirational. The guitar makes me smile, and the piano calms my nerves. The musicians are very talented and bring passion to every service. This is one of my direct sources of the universal consciousness.

After the service, people talk in a relaxed manner, and I have yet to be almost run over in the parking lot. Usually, I am driving the wrong way on a one-way drive; someone nicely waves me towards the exit in the right direction without anger or frustration. No one is in a rush to leave. When they do leave, they all have smiles on their faces.

I have found that the community-oriented churches of the city have this same feel. When I was an adolescent, we went to a community service after dropping off clothes or bakery goods. The congregants always started by taking the time to say good morning to those in the adjoining pews. It did not matter if you were rich or poor; we all stood as one, reverencing life. Labels did not infiltrate this small congregation; whether you slept outside on the steps of the church or you were blessed with an abundance of wealth, everyone was treated as an equal. Furthermore, when I taught in the inner city, the school was attached to a church that had one of the most wonderful Gospel choirs your ears have ever heard. The first time my wife and I went to a service, we were welcomed in the most compassionate way. It immediately felt like home.

If you are non-churchgoing, consider something as simple as a book club. My mother joined a book club a couple of years ago with some of my father's relatives. They get together once a month to discuss a book. Sometimes half of them haven't had time to read the selection; the more important aspect is spending this time enjoying each other's company.

On a visit this past weekend, my family met midway between Cleveland, Philadelphia, and Albany to celebrate my sister's birthday. Most of our trips entail all of us staring at Anna, my niece, as she plays; but this one took an interesting twist. We discussed the book I mentioned earlier, which my mom was reading during the visit, Rhonda Byrne's *The Secret*. It was nice to hear all the different perspectives of the same book. We gave our viewpoints, and I outlined this book to all who were involved. I felt accepted and thankful for the wonderful family I have. They welcomed my ideas by listening with intention. So much learning takes place when we verbalize our understandings of the universal truths.

Additionally, athletics are also a pastime that builds a sense of community. For example, running clubs go to different road races as teams and cheer each other on to new personal records. Men and women every spring, summer, and fall play softball, as if they were kids again, at local parks with their friends and family watching. As a kid, I remember going to my aunt and uncle's softball games, where there was laughing and joy in everyone's faces. They lost themselves in the moment and felt like kids at the sandlot.

Follow your own star!
—Dante Alighieri

Any activity you have joined that allows you to feel the group is more important than the individual is the sense community I am pointing towards. These are times you can forget your worries and take pleasure in being with a group of people you love. You just need to be involved in something that brings you together with people and allows you to have this sense of presence.

Our first apartment had a community pool that came alive every summer. People of all walks of life shared beers, had a few words, and discussed books; but more than anything, they made you feel at home. There was always someone to talk to at the pool, and no one was offended if you just wanted to catch a quick nap or get lost in a book. If you were playing a game or throwing the ball around, everyone joined in. Old, young, single, married, divorced, it did not matter; labels were not apparent.

The same process takes place on my college every spring. The first warm, sunny day, which may not even break seventy degrees, draws out crowds of people you never knew existed in such a small liberal arts school. Frisbees, barbecue, lacrosse sticks, and smiles welcome every new, warm spring day with laughter and happiness. This sense of community can take place anywhere people come together to celebrate the simple things in life. Join up, reconcile, and begin to live your life again with people who care to take the time just to enjoy your presence.

Awareness of a Higher Power

You will make your own path, but at its center needs to be the awareness of a higher power. What is God? I am not going to debate that issue because if I told you I knew, I would be the liar that most religious fanatics are. Belief is powerful and can come in many different forms; however, there appears to be some common truths that we all share.

There is a higher power that is beyond our understanding. You have felt it through the love of your child or the warmth in your heart that arose in a time of despair. Entering into this awakening of a higher power gives meaning in your life. Whether you believe it is Jesus, God, the Buddha, Shiva, or the Easter Bunny is all irrelevant to me. What is important is what direction it leads your life. Jesus spoke of peace on earth and an equality, which two thousand years later we are still working towards. The Buddha spoke of the end of suffering. These are noble challenges that fall into the practice of the third pillar of improving the quality of life around you.

I believe religion can be used in many ways. It can also be so falsely interpreted that it causes men to crash into towers filled with people of over eighty nationalities. It can be as blind as the Catholics were in the time of the Holocaust or as ignorant as any crusade, including the current Islamic terrorist attacks in the name of their unmerciful God. But I have found there is one truth for which we all are accountable: our responsibility to work towards fulfilling a need that is greater than our own as a celebration of the higher power.

Gestalt psychology, which originated in Germany, is based on the idea that the whole is greater than the sum of its parts. This concept should be applied to our lives because we are all intertwined in the largest fraternity in the world—humanity. Spirituality should help people be better than the mind has caused us to be. I will listen to any theory or belief system and give respect to its followers, even the ones that cause suffering; but I will not accept the lies and I will only see the truth of its teachings. I am practicing my eclectic faith in every breath I take. That faith is based on the idea that I will leave the world a better place than it was before I arrived. I reverence the beauty of this earth and the love we as humans are able to express in anyway we choose.

The consciousness of this power that runs through the universe and in every cell of your body enables us to be aware that we are not alone. This allows peace of mind. You may not believe the stories of the Bible or Koran, but the idea of someone watching over us is not so bad. When you feel this presence, it is even better.

My faith has been as inconsistent as a trip intoWashington, D.C. because you can never predict the traffic just as I can never predict where I will be on any given day in my path of accepting the truth. There is one theme that has always pulled me out of a rut: Although I can't control anything else in the world, I am responsible for all my actions. The fact that my wife and I were able to move back to her family in a couple of months without any major problems is beyond me. God or that all-encompassing life force in this world has a way of working in mysterious ways that are beyond my understanding.

I am at a point where I have stopped challenging the fact that the only thing that is certain is uncertainty; it has left me at peace with myself and the world. It allows me not to react to unconsciousness. That is why, when you are on top of your game, nothing can stop you. You stop listening to the voice in your head and become more positive. Everything seems to happen as if it was fate. You stop complaining and blaming. Once you realize you hold the key to your destiny, you can drive to any destination of your choosing.

I declare the truth and give thanks.
I am perfect as I am in this very moment.
I am beautiful, strong, unconditionally loved, and accepted.
I am _____.
And I am choosing to be happy today.

Thank you for this very breath.
Thank you for allowing me to practice.
Thank you for the abundance of wealth, relationships,
and well-being in the world.
Thank you for _____.

I close my eyes and envision
My dream.
I see myself achieving my goal to become a Renaissance *Man or Woman*
And to _____.
I visualize my newly fulfilled life.

I feel
The gift of this dream and my goal becoming a reality,
The one loving consciousness, which flows through our universe,
Full of unconditional love and acceptance
And this abundance of *(God)* energy.

Celebrate.
Smile.
Have fun
and feel the joy of living.
I give thanks for receiving all of this.
I give thanks for my greater purpose and the overall balance in my life.
And I give thanks for _____.

I declare
My purpose, established by
(God, a higher power, or the universe)
Is to spread unconditional love and acceptance through

_____.

I will constantly be reborn to this moment
without memory or judgment.
I will share all my wealth, relationships, and overall well-being
to improve the quality of life around me.
My *(day, evening, or* _____.*)* will be enjoyable and fulfilling!

Chapter 7

Running or Walking the Stress Out of Your Life

Opening the Mind to New Possibilities

Running and nature open the mind to infinite possibilities. Every day my mind expands to a greater depth. This is a direct effect of the beauty of nature because this is the world's purpose. Your life is a manifestation of the universe's expression of itself. As you run through nature, you reconnect with the consciousness of God. I learned this from a young man who I befriended in my first year of teaching. I shared my passion of running with my students; and after one of my students saw me run, something truly special transpired.

Tom started asking about my running. I was surprised that he was so interested, and I told him that I would take him for a jog one day if he wanted to go. I thought he was only kidding because in the city there are very few things that matter to young minds. Most revolve around one game, basketball; but sure enough, he was serious. He wanted to run.

However, we couldn't run in the neighborhood after school because it was not safe for the kids, let alone for an African-American boy and his white teacher together. One day I received directions to a park that had a trail around a stream. We left school and after a five-to ten-minute ride had an instant transformation from the city to the suburbs as we entered an affluent part of the city where there were nice homes and the park.

Tom had never been to this particular park. I couldn't believe he lived so close and had never been to such a beautiful place. I learned that in the city you don't leave your neighborhood because it is all you know. Consequently, I can still remember the day we ran for the first time and Tom's words, "I can finally breathe out here." His face lit up when we ran! Right then and there, I saw the power of running in nature.

We started the first day just running a mile. As the Thursday runs continued, he grew more confident in himself. His running and mind began to transform. He was reborn to the utter beauty of the world. We occasionally sprinted just to have some fun. On our final trip, we just sat next to the water. He said he could do homework all day just sitting and watching the water. I could see the peace in his eyes, which were usually filled with fear.

Running is a powerful tool to strengthen a man's will to overcome all obstacles. I am glad I had the experience of running with Tom because running released the tension that had been building up in both of us. I could see him growing as he ran around the trail, a smile on his face, releasing his lungs that had been trapped for so long. This pillar has so much power in opening people up to what was previously unknown and creates new possibilities in their lives. As I continue to run on a new trail, my ideas for this book become clearer and more distinct.

> *Human subtlety will never devise an invention more beautiful, more simple, or more direct than does Nature, because in her inventions, nothing is lacking and nothing is superfluous.*
> —*Leonardo Da Vinci*

A Cold Saturday Morning

It is January during one of the mildest winters I have ever encountered since I was a kid, but after checking the weather I realize it is thirty degrees. However, it feels like eighteen. After spending a year down South, that is pretty cold for my liking. I put on my Under Armor shirt, fleece-hooded sweatshirt, jacket, spandex running pants, polyester warm-ups, ear muffs, winter hat, and gloves; then I tie my hood tight. As you can see, I have become a little soft after a year in Atlanta. I used to run only wearing a jacket and one pair of pants. I can hear the wind punishing my apartment building; but it is Saturday, my favorite day of the week for my run and corresponding walking meditation.

I start off slowly. As soon as my feet hit the pavement, my insides feel like ice. I can feel my knees pounding into the solid concrete. I wish I had put on a thick pair of shorts in between layers because the worst cold is in the place right between your legs. The cold hits it like a knife through the skin. Then it happens as it always does: A laugh sneaks out of my lungs. Then another giggle. The sun is shining and I am ready for a run.

As I move through the neighborhood, I wonder why I am the only one out here. Then the wind hits me again, causing me to break my stride. This answers my question. Nonetheless, I am as happy as can be. A little more laughter escapes at the thought, the kind of laughter you couldn't control when you were a teenager at church or a child who gazed at his first rainbow in glee, the uncontrollable, innocent kind. It happens when I run. I don't know why. Maybe it's those natural endorphins people are always talking about.

Now that I am out of the neighborhood, I find my way onto the path. My mind flutters off. Ideas for this book appear, questions about teaching flash by, and solutions to problems are answered. Ten minutes later, I can hear the flow of the stream that is parallel to my path and the birds that are so calming. I used to need my MP3 player to run more than a few miles, but now I only need to hear the sound of the trail as I run.

> *Nature is the art of God.*
> *—Dante Alighieri*

A car flies by. I unconsciously greet another runner, some walkers, and the stream again; then the wind wakes me up. My mind makes its last effort to control my attention, but I have finished half my run. Since it is Saturday, I take the time to walk along the creek for some relaxation. Oops, I almost run into another runner. I didn't even know she was there, but she doesn't mind because she knows what all runners know: We are all addicted and in a trance.

Glasser described the process as positive addiction, which is also the title of his book. Our state of mind is hypnotized, and we are pleasantly empty. My practice was not as consistent until I read his book. I realized the lethargic feeling I felt in the past was not from running too much but from not keeping up the practice as I do now (1976).

I am completely relaxed. I break stride to begin my walk and feel my inner body in my hands. They feel like thick pillows. I follow my inhalation to the pause in my lower abdomen and back up through the lungs. Out my nose comes the breath and I begin again. Then I hear it all again: the birds, the water, the silence of the trees. I see the sun's rays, some more people, another runner, and again a car wakes me up.

It is cold. I realize that I am going to cut this walk short. That is okay because I have tomorrow and every day after. More important-ly, I have Saturdays for the rest of my life for the daily run and this meditative walk. The wind feels nicer on my back. The thick pillows and the awareness of my breath return. I am lost again. The feeling spreads through my body and into my heart. I am at peace. Nature has yet again awakened me to the universal consciousness. My whole body feels alive. Then I go back to a jog and emptiness.

Ten minutes later I am almost back to the development, the last hill. Oops, the wind hits me so hard I break stride. This isn't going to be easy. The wind has picked up, and somehow I am running right into it again. Okay, here comes the challenge. I am awake now. The wind is blowing and I have lost my positive addiction. I focus. Lift your chest, pick up those feet, keep your hands swinging, don't cross them, smile, you can do it. Four more intersections. Three more. Keep your focus. You are getting lazy; pick up those feet, shoulders back, try to make them touch. Two more. Look, the last part of the hill. Don't slouch. That wind is cold. You there, let the car pass.

Now it's all down hill. Ease into it. The store fronts, a mother and her son. Stop running and enjoy another walk. The chill of the sweat I have accumulated distracts my breathing. Another laugh. People must think I am crazy. The pillows are back. Swinging back and forth makes you feel alive. Relaxation. My favorite tree. What is that tow truck doing? Another large gust, a giggle. Now I know I am crazy. Contentment, acceptance, and an overall awareness of the inner body returns peace to my heart. I am at ease; the stresses of my life fade into the background. Hey, there is the guy from Cleveland that asked about my car. I have done it, another successful run.

Take off the gloves. Get up the stairs. Don't take off too much at once. I am so cold. Get the Under Armor shirt off; it is drenched. Put your sweatshirt back on. The water feels so good running down my throat. I need another glass. Lie down; put your butt against the wall, your legs up, and just relax. That is why I run and why I can't stop running. It's healthy, enjoyable, and challenging.

Unhealthy Motives to a Worthy Practice

There are many reasons for beginning this worthy practice, but let's take a look at some reasons that you should not use for motivation. These are to lose weight, to make your body look better, to increase speed, to compete, or to prove anything. These reasons rip the passion and beauty out of the process. The first few weeks back I had to wear a watch so I could run for thirty-five minutes as I had planned; but once the routine and course was in place, there was no more watch, just me, my shoes, the sound of the running water, the pavement, and the laughing.

> **The Proven Power of Running**
> *Aerobic exercise, in the absence of weight loss, can improve insulin sensitivity, which will decrease your risk of getting diabetes.*
> *Kirwan et al, 1990*

I have to make a plan, or I get too excited and run myself into another injury. So I set myself for thirty-five minutes of running and ten minutes of walking, unless it is Saturday when my walk takes much longer. I never increase my running unless I plan to do so, although the walking may be increased at anytime. As spring and summer arrive, the nice weather increases my time out in nature.

However, in late February, a snow storm and the cold sentenced me to end my outdoor runs. Snow days are wonderful for a teacher, but they are not so great for a runner. The path is completely covered and the streets are icy, which means I am off the path and in the gym.

Oh, the noise, the television, the chattering, the distractions! Although my body was somewhat nourished by the elliptical, treadmill, and bike, my mental state suffered. Running releases stress, which is embedded in our souls; the synapses that become disoriented realign during a nice jog. In the gym, I feel so trapped I have to distract myself with my MP3 player, which at that time was broken. I fell subject to whoever was working out, and I could not find the natural flow I feel during my runs. I do not run with a watch outside because the time is irrelevant to the practice. On the treadmill, however, time plagues me. How many minutes? I only have been going for five. I am so bored. These are just a few of the thoughts that overtake my mind. I have to be so much more aware of my ego to battle it from overtaking all I have worked to gain control of during my practices.

I rarely laugh when I am in the gym. Contrastingly, on the path, I am oblivious to the world. I can laugh, smile, and even sing; but when I'm in the gym, I'm concerned with how I look and so many other distractions. I think about the other people on the treadmills. I try not to listen to the moms criticizing teachers, and I try not to be overcome by my thoughts. Oh, the day I had to listen to Rachel Ray compare washing spaghetti sauces off two different painted cabinets and testing of the durability of some bras, I wanted to scream. I had never before seen the show. It might be great; but when you just want to run, it is the last thing you want to watch.

> *My soul can find no staircase to Heaven unless it be through Earth's loveliness.*
> *—Michelangelo*

The only way I can prevent the take over of my consciousness is if I bring my music or I read. I edited some of my work while I was on the elliptical. This was the only cure I could find for the dreadful gym. Consequently, next year I have already decided to trudge through the snow to avoid this insanity. Be aware and stay away unless this is your last resort.

Now think of the boy in the city whose only chance was to run with his teacher who left him for a better life. He just wanted to breathe, but the city prevented him. What is your excuse because I can no longer think of one?

In grade school, my coach told me I would never sprint in high school because I did not have the natural ability needed to be successful. I am glad he told me that. He was a wonderful man, and he probably didn't even realize that he spoke so negatively. What an inspiration that was for me to become successful! By the end of my high school career, I had met my best friend Aaron, who has always been a perfect compliment to me. Together we ran on a relay team and broke a couple of records. I was the slowest on the team, but I got us off on the right foot. However, this is not the type of running that I am suggesting. I was motivated to run to prove someone wrong and to be the best. I was overly critical of myself and spent way too much time in the weight room.

> **The Proven Power of Running**
> *A study showed there is a reduced risk of cardiovascular problems and obesity from decreased blood pressure as well as many other benefits that have been confirmed by the study of individuals who consistently exercise in moderation. In addition, they are less prone to injury and sickness because of their improved glucose tolerance, lipid profile, and immune systems.*
> *Adamu et al, 2006*

After taking years off from running because of a dislocated shoulder, I began running my senior year in college. I ran for about twenty minutes a day for a week straight, but I made the mistake of calling my sister in celebration. Within six weeks, I was running a marathon.

My sister is an amazing person. When I say she is overly ambitious, I mean this as the highest compliment. She convinced me that I should run the Cleveland Marathon. I went from never running over six miles to running up to nineteen miles in the limited time before the marathon. My sister knew exactly what to say to make me achieve more than I ever thought possible. She convinced me that because I had a high VO2max, I would be an awesome marathon runner. What is a VO2max? I am not really sure although I know it has something to do with how you are able to use oxygen.

My wife and sister both received their master's degrees from the same school in the same program. All the tests I avoided by being away at college when my sister was earning her master's, my wife made me complete when it was her turn to complete her degree. I was poked, prodded, weighed, put in machines that looked like space ships, had wires attached to me, and wore breathing apparatuses to help my wife practice her technical skills. One of them required me to run on a treadmill with an oxygen mask attached to a tube connected to some machine that basically pushed me to my limits, literally to the point I was falling off the elevated treadmill.

After the test, I called my sister to tell her about it because I knew she would be more than interested. This conversation led me to achieving what I thought was an impossible task. I thank her for pushing me where I would have never gone without her support.

> **The Proven Power of Running**
>
> *After a 10k road race, over twenty long distance runners positively increased their mood from the beginning of the run. This was further seen by the amplification of beta-endorphin-like immunoreactivity, which was studied at the end of the race.*
>
> *Wildman et al, 1986*

The marathon was the first time I had ever reached positive addiction. This has been coined the runner's high by some; but after walking two miles because of the pain in my knee, I finished the last three miles faster than any of the other twenty-three. I was so giddy I just started laughing and sprinting by all the people who had seen my dreadful face in the previous miles as they passed me by. When my wife was running with me for the last eight hundred meters, I realized I was at the finish line and sprinted past her to complete the marathon.

I immediately collapsed. The massage therapist gave me an extra twenty minutes because of the torture I had put my body through. I remember cringing as each knot was worked out of my body. The line grew longer and longer as I lay and was treated, but I could have cared less. The rest of the day was quite painful, and the agony of the following month convinced me never to recommend training for a marathon in less than six months. This again is not the running of the Renaissance Man, although I am not discouraging anyone from running a marathon. Just don't make the same dumb mistake I made by training only for six weeks.

The Benefits of This Pillar

On the other hand, my mother followed a friend's suggestion and began to walk after she divorced my father. She walked her way into a new marriage when she found Bob, who had lived right across the street for over thirty years. She walked every day for approximately an hour on a course she created around the neighborhood. It unwound her mind, I believe, and helped her release the stress in her life. She appeared healthier than I could ever remember, and there was so much excitement in her eyes. I saw it reduce some of her pain, which used to trail along. She had regained a lost strength and looked as if she was ready to take on the world again. It was fun to listen to her talk about walking. It was like her little baby, who she was so proud of. She felt better because walking, like running, is another form of meditation. She found peace in her life by walking.

Ironically, my father has been transformed by walking as well. He loves Huntington Beach and talks of the peace it brings to his life. I usually call my father; but when he does call, it is from Huntington Beach. I can hear it in his voice, the calmness and joy, which are direct effects of walking in nature. I love receiving those phone calls when his love is overflowing on to the trail and he feels he needs to share it with his family. He

> **The Proven Power of Running**
> *The Diabetes Prevention Program Research Group (DPPRG) reported a 58% lower incidence of Type 2 diabetes after diet and exercise interventions.*
> *DPPRG 2002*

seems whole again. He knows it is his therapy to cleanse his life of all its sorrows and his rejection. His mind is at ease, and he does not let it overtake him as he walks on the beach. He awakens to the utter beauty of nature.

As children, we all ran as if there were no tomorrow. A child knows that running is fun. Our ancestors hunted for survival, and it is this innate nature to run that is so appealing to so many people.

The choice that needs to be made is either to run or to walk at the appropriate level your body can handle. This means consulting your family physician. Ideally, if you could run or walk five to seven days a week, you will become positively addicted in less than two years, as Glasser explains (1976). I find that running thirty-five minutes is the perfect amount for me, and I walk after I run for a ten-minute cool down.

Begin with fifteen minutes of walking and running and only add a minute each week to reach your ideal time. There is no rush because you will be practicing for the rest of your life. Use your body as your guide. If it is hurting, reduce the time. Give it the appropriate rest it needs, but don't stop walking or running because of fatigue. The mind is just trying to trick you into quitting. However, if you become injured, be sure to rest and heal for the appropriate amount of time recommended by your doctor.

Some Helpful Tips to Start

I have awakened to some truths from past mistakes and my current success of a pain-free practice. While running, I attempt to focus on my breath as I do in meditation. I also try to improve my form, working on my posture and picking up my feet to attempt to reduce the pounding on my knees. It is a practice that should be done independently.

Although I run with my wife on Sundays, I find that doing so anymore than that is not healthy. When my wife began running and meditating, it was difficult for me to adjust. I stopped running at one point because of an injury she had, as I discussed earlier. I strongly suggest this is something you do on your own with some planned walks or runs with others along the way. My mother also fell prey to this when she began walking with her husband Bob. When he was not able to continue, she stopped and now only walks occasionally. If you want to walk or run with someone, make those outings additional to the normal practice for this pillar.

Also, do not judge your running. Allow yourself time to improve, but never focus on your speed or do any road races in the early part of your practice. Walk or run just for the enjoyment.

Running increases the release of natural endorphins, it helps control appetite, and it is a healthy exercise when done in moderation. If your body is not capable of running, then walk. If you can only run for a ten minutes to begin, then run ten minutes; but do not let your ego sabotage your practice. This practice is something you do just for the sake of being healthier. The positive effects of running can navigate your life back into the right direction.

For further learning in this practice, Danny Dreyer writes and teaches his approach in *Chi Running: A Revolutionary Approach to Effortless, Injury-Free Running.* I have successfully incorporated some of his teachings in my running. So many runners are plagued with knee, feet, hip, and back problems. Dreyer explains in depth four chi skills: focusing the mind, body sensing, breathing, and relaxation. This style of running is based on a slanted posture, creating the least resistance on the bones and muscles to prevent injuries (2004).

Becoming aware of your body when you are running, using some of the meditative techniques previously mentioned, and allowing yourself to relax into the run alleviate stress and cleanse your mind of disorderly thoughts running rampantly through your brain. Just have fun!

I declare the truth and give thanks.
I am perfect as I am in this very moment.
I am beautiful, strong, unconditionally loved, and accepted.
I am _____.
And I am choosing to be happy today.

Thank you for this very breath.
Thank you for allowing me to practice.
Thank you for the abundance of wealth, relationships,
and well-being in the world.
Thank you for _____.

I close my eyes and envision
My dream.
I see myself achieving my goal to become a Renaissance *Man or Woman*
And to _____.
I visualize my newly fulfilled life.

I feel
The gift of this dream and my goal becoming a reality,
The one loving consciousness, which flows through our universe,
Full of unconditional love and acceptance
And this abundance of *(God)* energy.

Celebrate.
Smile.
Have fun
and feel the joy of living.
I give thanks for receiving all of this.
I give thanks for my greater purpose and the overall balance in my life.
And I give thanks for _____.

I declare
My purpose, established by
(God, a higher power, or the universe)
Is to spread unconditional love and acceptance through
_____.

I will constantly be reborn to this moment
without memory or judgment.
I will share all my wealth, relationships, and overall well-being
to improve the quality of life around me.
My *(day, evening, or* _____.*)* will be enjoyable and fulfilling!

Additional Suggested Resources

Glasser, William. *The Positive Addiction.* New York: Perennial Library, 1976.

This is a great book to read to understand the importance of positive addictions such as running, yoga, and meditation. It has helped me realize why I love these practices but also why at times I have stopped running, meditating, or practicing yoga. This is also where I gained the idea of how to gain strength from these practices to overcome my own weaknesses by continuing these addictions and increasing my strength exponentially.

Dreyer, Danny, & Dreyer, Katherine. *Chi Running: A Revolutionary Approach to Effortless, Injury-Free Running.* Fireside, NY: Simon & Schuster, 2004.

As described in the book, this is a running style which Danny Dreyer has created for life-long practice without any problems. He teaches you how to enjoy running as a child does without injury or strain. He has a wealth of knowledge in running with no boundaries.

Chapter 8

Creativity: A Means to Liberation

The Unbelievable Influence of Dance

Creativity has a very powerful effect on people; it empowers you to be in the present moment, which is priceless. I will contrast my adolescence with my wife's to prove how powerful this pillar is. As a youth, I was very discontent with life, as are many adolescents and young adults. I had supportive friends, helpful siblings, and caring parents. I was always an A or B+ student, and I was successful in sports. However, none of those had any great value in my life. Like most youth, I felt life was pointless. I lacked self-acceptance. None of my activities had the powerful effect apparent in my wife's life in high school.

> A beautiful thing never gives so much pain as does failing to hear and see it.
> —Michelangelo

When I was at a party on a Tuesday night over consuming substances, Ashley was helping some four-year-old with her first position. As my night progressed, I avoided the present moment at any cost, consuming whatever I could get my hands on. She was improving pirouettes, completely aware of her body and the moment. As my night wound to an end and I was thinking of how to sneak past my mother without any repercussions from my actions, she arrived home to study and complete her homework while stretching on the floor. If you had asked me why I was drinking at the time, I would have given some either cynical or philosophical rant about the inadequacies of the world. On the other hand, if you had asked my wife why she wasn't, she would have said, "I don't know. I hadn't thought about it." She would not have debated. Unlike most adults, she had found what we are all looking for—self-acceptance. She was content with her life.

How powerful is dance? Let's think of what it has empowered Ashley to do. She taught dance in high school to pay for her dance classes; she took responsibility. She graduated at the top of her pre-med class in college, where she also took dance as her minor. She received full-paid tuition for her master's degree at one of the top universities in the country, along with a stipend. She is completing her doctorate, having received another scholarship. She still works in the studio where she began dancing twenty years ago. Her dance teacher, Miss Cathy, was in our wedding. That is the power of creativity. She related not with the ego but with pure consciousness, while I was incessantly thinking and controlled by my ego. She was doing this without effort, which is what true Renaissance Men and Women are able to accomplish. It was not until I went through counseling and began meditating that I was able to achieve such accomplishments. The paths of Renaissance Men take many forms, but what they should all have in common is the practices that reduce incessant thinking and increase active engagement. This strength obtained will lead to accomplishment and contentment.

> **The Proven Power of Dance**
> *Dance improved the quality of life of breast cancer patients by meeting their physical and emotional needs.*
> Sandel et al, 2005

A Delicate Passage Through a Windy Road

My practice of this pillar has had its ups and downs through the years. It is the practice I continually try to improve. During a busy week, I have thoughts of painting. When I am lost in my mind and feel sorry for myself, I usually do not respond to this thought. Then I feel this emptiness, which makes me feel lethargic. Something is missing in my life when I am not using my creativity. Usually I am so entrenched in my mind during these periods that I am unaware of the problem. However, my heart finds a means to the resolution, and I find the brush in my hand. I am complete again.

When I am painting, peace runs through my veins and I am content until my ego trickles back into my mind. Then I begin to force the strokes onto the canvas until I settle back into the vision and allow it to take me away. Time sneaks by; hours pass. I am the brush, the canvas, and the creation. Joy spreads through my body and healing begins. I begin with a background that sets the tone for the painting. It may be chaotic at first, but it slowly calms down. Once the backdrop has been laid, I discover the direction of the painting and build it from the center out. A surge takes place that gives my painting purpose. I add the finishing touches. At last comes my favorite part: I give my art to another person as an act of love.

> *Every child is an artist. The problem is how to remain an artist once you grow up.*
> —Pablo Picasso

When we are children, it is so easy to see what gifts we have to offer. We constantly practice those gifts until someone tells us we are not good at them or we begin to self-judge our work. As a child, I loved drawing. This continued through school until I was a senior in high school when I decided I might become an artist. I literally spent half of the day in the art room. My art teacher allowed me to do this and work undisturbed. Occasionally, I changed between the three art rooms because a class was too full for me to occupy the entire table I needed to work.

> *Where the spirit does not work with the hand, there is no art.*
> —Leonardo Da Vinci

Then I lost my love. I began to listen to my ego and its incessant thinking. I thought I lacked skill and I began to lose my creativity. I became overly critical of my artwork and myself. Although painting did not have the power that dancing had on my wife, it was truly therapeutic during this difficult time.

An Act of Love That Has the Power to Heal

Art has healed so many emotional wounds in my life. I find that I am the most content in front of an easel as long as I am painting for kids, my mom, Ashley, her mom, Anna, or anyone else. We all need that peace that comes through creativity, more now than ever in the craziness of the modern lifestyle.

I was lucky that I had this much time to practice without fear. Beyond my own self-criticisms that distorted my art, I had a couple of college professors who made art into a science, which it can never be. I thought that was my last straw with painting; but after working in a gallery, I rekindled my passion, although I know my love for Ashley was what truly brought the brush back into my hand.

The summer only months after I met my future wife, I was so in love I drove twelve hours just to see her on a whim that she could be the one. I had never driven over an hour and a half by myself and thought that was an all-day trip. With some coercion from Domenico, I got in the car and just drove. I actually enjoyed most of the ride.

Ashley told me she lived in Philadelphia, but that was not exactly the truth. I passed lovely manure-scented fields where cows grazed. Then I pulled up to the driveway where her parents sat on their rocking chairs. They said hello with a smile and all the rest is history. They accepted me into their lives with open arms.

The Proven Power of Art
Cancer patients began to make connections to others not based on illness but on similarities in their creative practices. This gave them more purpose maintaining previous interests, increased relationships through positive interactions with other patients, and gave them confidence from overcoming creative challenges.

Reynolds et al, 2006

Ashley and I went to the park and then to a little Italian place. I felt even more nervous, thinking that I should not have come because it was too crazy and she probably thought I was crazy. Well, I was out of my mind and that is what she thought, but she was so happy that I came. This is clear evidence that love has no logic or borders; it is silly and innocent.

A couple of months later, I created what one of my best friends Derek said was the finest canvas he had ever seen me paint. This meant a great deal to me because he is straight forward and to the point. I painted Tinkerbell for Ashley's birthday. While it cannot even come close to the beauty of my wife, it is breathtaking. That painting has hung in our apartment to this very day. Ashley has inspired me to paint and accomplish great things. She has helped me write this book; and with her love, she will inspire me to do even more.

As a kid, I lived in a perfect house, the one that always had its door open. I think half my friends loved coming over just for my mom's cooking. My mother still lives on that street but on the other side with her husband Bob. She inspired me to paint a watercolor of our home in autumn. I gave this painting as an act of love. It hangs across the street from the house, which is now painted another color but still holds all the memories.

Finally, inspired by Anna, was a painting of Winnie the Pooh, Tigger, Piglet, and the rest of the gang. My niece, who at the time was celebrating her first Christmas, has been a blessing in our family's life. Her big, blue eyes light up the room and you can tell she is taking it all in, one experience at a time. Every time I see Anna, my heart leaps out of my chest. I was able to capture this feeling right on the canvas.

An Unexpected Gift at an Unexpected Time

My brother found his peace in writing, beginning late in his college years. He has since transitioned from writing films to writing poetry. This is his solitude. He loves to wake up in the morning and write as he did in college. When you watch him when he is in front of his computer, you truly see the wonderful person who sits before you. His life pours right onto the paper; his poetry is as honest and innocent as a child. His words have helped so many close friends when they needed it most.

Art owes its origin to Nature herself...this beautiful creation, the world, supplied the first model, while the original teacher was that divine intelligence which has not only made us superior to the other animals, but like God Himself, if I may venture to say it.

—Giorgio Vasari

During my sophomore year in college, a very close friend to us, Jenine, died in a freak accident. Greg, my brother's roommate the previous year, had invested all that mattered into Jenine. She was the high school prom queen and then an actress in college. She was always in the spotlight and even more so when she performed. She had a way about her that made the people around her feel important. When she died, all of us were empty. I was not as close as Greg and my brother were to her, but still I struggled with her death until I heard Billy's words. Greg was giving one of the two eulogies at the funeral. He is quite the talker, and we expected him to have much to say. Everyone waited to hear his words and for him to articulate what Jenine meant to him. Instead, he read something someone else had written as a gift of condolence to him. Billy, my brother, told the story as it should be told. He wrote a poem about how Jenine spread love in every breath. She lived every moment to its fullest potential and with so much excitement. She expressed this love by sharing it with everyone in her life.

> **The Proven Power of Creativity**
> *Over 65 percent of the members of a study felt using their creative ability had improved their well-being and quality of life during rehabilitation*
>
> Batt-Rawden et al, 2005

A Means of Self-exploration and Personal Expression

Creativity is such an important pillar because of the positive benefits you acquire from it. You find yourself through expressing creativity. My wife began dancing at the age of three, and she danced through her college years. First, it gave her purpose. She began to improve herself with limited destructive criticism. Dancing teaches students discipline and the work ethic and allows them to challenge themselves mentally and emotionally. Until the point where judgment comes into play, it is one of the healthiest practices you can have.

I have passionately enjoyed entertaining children ever since I can remember. In the classroom, I do not see what I do as teaching.

I am more of an actor on a stage, and the teaching is secondary. My knowledge in the field of education enables me to stand in front of students and just let loose. My lessons are not well-planned scripts but a spontaneous stand-up hour. I invent crazy stories while teaching the concepts of mathematics and conduct Jeopardy review games before challenging tests. I am sure public speakers feel the same way; give me a topic and an audience and that is all I need.

Creativity is a pillar we cannot afford to waste. All people should have a creative outlet. Find yours. Brainstorm right now all the things you loved to do as a child. Then pick one to start. It may involve taking a class for photography, dancing, creative writing, or drama. You may choose, as I have, to be self-motivated and just practice in your house. You may begin to write as I have, or overcome your fear of the stage and sing in your choir at church or in a musical at the local theater. Whatever craft you choose, begin this moment because it is a choice you cannot afford to pass.

> *When there is no vision, people perish.*
> *—Proverbs 29:18 KJV*

If you can't find an outlet on your own, begin to draw. Betty Edwards is a world renowned teacher; her book *Drawing From the Right Side of Brain* has taught thousands of people who have never drawn to use art as an outlet for their busy lives. She will take the fear away from the practice. If you find yourself still wavering, try Julia Cameron's elegant book *The Artist's Way: A Spiritual Path to Higher Creativity,* which has the power to help you find your path in the creative arts.

You have been given these gifts by the universe, God, or family members as I have. You need to thank them through practicing and sharing them with all. I am forever thankful for the ability I have acquired from my father and grandfather, who both were professional artists. Their practice has continued in my own. Creativity has brought my wife to this state of pure consciousness. It has the power to heal the world of all its pain and suffering.

I declare the truth and give thanks.
I am perfect as I am in this very moment.
I am beautiful, strong, unconditionally loved, and accepted.
I am _____.
And I am choosing to be happy today.

Thank you for this very breath.
Thank you for allowing me to practice.
Thank you for the abundance of wealth, relationships,
and well-being in the world.
Thank you for _____.

I close my eyes and envision
My dream.
I see myself achieving my goal to become a Renaissance *Man or Woman*
And to _____.
I visualize my newly fulfilled life.

I feel
The gift of this dream and my goal becoming a reality,
The one loving consciousness, which flows through our universe,
Full of unconditional love and acceptance
And this abundance of *(God)* energy.

Celebrate.
Smile.
Have fun
and feel the joy of living.
I give thanks for receiving all of this.
I give thanks for my greater purpose and the overall balance in my life.
And I give thanks for _____.

I declare
My purpose, established by
(God, a higher power, or the universe)
Is to spread unconditional love and acceptance through

_____.

I will constantly be reborn to this moment
without memory or judgment.
I will share all my wealth, relationships, and overall well-being
to improve the quality of life around me.
My *(day, evening, or* _____.*)* will be enjoyable and fulfilling!

Additional Suggested Resources

Cameron, Julia. *The Artist's Way: A Spiritual Path to Higher Creativity.* Los Angeles: Jeremy P. Tarcher/Perigee, 1992.
I have found this to be a reawakening of my creativity I had as a child. She allows you to reflect on your creativity in such an accepting manner. It will enable you to awaken to what has been lost. You will regain your awareness and creativity.

Edwards, Betty. *Drawing on the Artist Within.* New York: Simon and Schuster, 1986.

Drawing on the Right Side of the Brain. New York: Jeremy P. Tarcher/Putman, 1999.
Both of her books allow anyone to become a very talented artist no matter what the previous experience or skill. She is inviting and empowers all to draw as we see. This is a great book for anyone who would like to use drawing as a creative outlet.

Chapter 9

The Culminating Practice of Yoga

Serendipity: A Truly Fortunate Accident

After learning about the law of attraction, I don't believe in chance. I call this a fortunate accident only because I believe my rebirth and new found awareness brought yoga to my life. It was days after our second Christmas as a married couple. My wife and I still had $40 left on our Best Buy gift card. I had already received all that I could think of, and we were aimlessly looking around for something to catch our attention. I saw a three disc yoga DVD collection and thought I recognized the name on the cover. I have no idea how that might have been possible because I knew very little about yoga at that point. I picked it up, put it down, walked around, couldn't find anything, and then finally got over my silly feeling and bought the DVDs. A million different egoic thoughts ran through my head with the same theme; all were reasons not to buy the DVDs. I was a guy. I liked lifting weights and thought of myself as tough. Why would I want yoga? Finally, I overcame this egoic onslaught and bought the set.

It may have been that day or a week later that I decided to try one of the videos with my wife. I have no athletic prowess by any means; my body has many limits. Even so, I could never have predicted how out of shape I felt trying to complete the video. My wife with her flexibility gained new respect from me, and I lost a little in my own ability. Then I realized how trivial it all was, and I began to laugh. There was no way that my body was going to finish this video. The more I tried, the harder I laughed. I was in hysterics. That was when I realized this must be some powerful stuff. I couldn't control my laughter; it was infectious, overtaking my body. Then I felt nothing, and then I was exhausted.

I have always loved to exercise. I was a pretty avid weight lifter in high school and college; I loved the feeling of pushing myself. When I benched three hundred pounds in high school, I wanted to push for more. With lifting, you are never content. Lifting also leaves your body in an unhealthy state when you do not practice in moderation or without stretching before and after. As a lifter, you get tighter and tighter, basically binding your muscles in a restraining manner. I had previously attempted yoga from reading about it and watching some of my wife's workout videos, but it was not until I bought this DVD collection by Rodney Yee that my practice really began.

Yoga has allowed me to love myself unconditionally. It has taught me how to feel. Although in the beginning I was concerned with my form, I have left this silliness in the past. As I felt I was getting weaker and losing muscle mass, I really became self-critical; but as my practice developed, I realized how much better I felt compared to my past experience of lifting.

The Proven Power of Yoga
The practice of yoga improved the quality of life of participants in the study. It also decreased cholesterol and blood pressure, as well as triglycerides of the participants in this group.
Damodaran et al, 2002

In lifting, you are constantly tracking how much you lift, judging yourself, and looking in the mirror. Most of the time you arrogantly like what you see, but eventually you are not satisfied. That is why so many people take supplements and why some fall victim to the use of performance-enhancing drugs. You are not big enough; you compare yourself to the other guys in the room. This builds your ego, but then someone walks in who creates doubt in your mind. Your thoughts begin to wander and you separate from who you are. You create an idea of perfection and work towards this illusion. Once you have this picture in your mind, you have created a divide. There is now an external goal in mind that leads to rejecting your body as it is. You think you are worthless or that you will be happier when you reach your goal.

The problem is you reject yourself when you should love your body unconditionally. The truth is you will never reach this idea of

perfection. Stop looking in the mirror for someone else and start seeing the beauty that life has created. Your body needs to be nourished
with exercise, but you need to choose a healthy supportive practice.

Devoting Yourself to the Practice

To be successful in this pillar, you do not need to master any poses.
All you have to do is devote yourself to practicing every day. That is
it! As I mentioned earlier in this book, I am not naturally
flexible; this has made yoga a challenge. With the help of my practice
at home, I have begun to open up without worrying about anything
but my breath.

I suggest beginning with yoga videos because if you really want
to have change in your life, you need to practice daily. Most people
cannot afford to practice yoga with a teacher on a daily basis. The
teachers who you may find in your local studios may be experts, but
they also may be people certified with no more than a month of
formal training. In addition, the commute and the preparation alone
are very difficult to overcome to practice daily at a studio. Buying a
set of videos can start you off inexpensively and allow you to build
from there. In the videos, you work with some of the best teachers in
the world every day in the comfort of your home.

All you need is to set aside some time and buy a yoga mat. At
Wal-Mart, you can buy a mat, blocks, and a band for less than $15.
The mat will help your balance, the blocks are props to help in
difficult poses, and the band helps increase flexibility in certain
positions. If you want to buy higher quality materials, Gaiam is one
of the leading yoga distributors. Mats and other props can be bought
online from their webpage, at your local Barnes & Noble, or at Dicks
Sporting Goods, among other stores that carry exercise equipment.

There are probably some awesome instructors in your general
area who can take your practice to another level, but is this necessary?
Probably not. If you are driven to find one, however, you should look.

Don't worry about anything as you begin. Just start. Slowly your
form will improve without effort and you will slowly use your breath
as a catalyst during the process. Make sure you rest your body in one
of the two different forms of child's pose whenever you are feeling
exhausted, your breathing is not relaxed, or you cannot perform a

difficult pose. Do not force the practice; allow it to blossom like a flower, naturally as the universe intended.

Because I came into yoga from sports and lifting, I wanted to perfect the poses. This is ironic because there is no perfect pose. When you begin, follow the directions for breathing techniques given by Ronald Yee in his videos; then work towards improving the pose. My breathing, as I began, sounded as if I was struggling to lift a car above my head because of the difficulty I had in attempting the poses. I should have allowed the breathing to come before worrying about correct alignment in the poses; I wasted much effort in trying poses that were beyond my ability, forcing my body as I did in lifting. However, in yoga, this is counterproductive.

Yoga block and mat

In yoga, your body achieves its goal when it is relaxed instead of being tensed as in lifting. This was a major struggle for me, and it may be difficult for you as well. Just have patience with yourself, and accept your body as it is in that moment. You have to approach yoga with a sense of humor because unless you are a dancer, more than likely your sessions won't be pretty. You need to give maximum effort without worrying if you are doing it right. The focus and dedication of the practice are similar to meditation. The important part is just get-

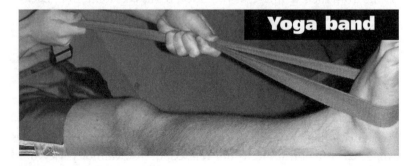

Yoga band

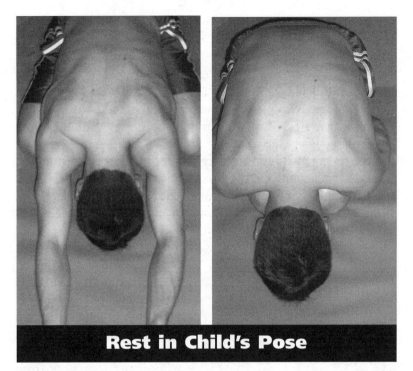

Rest in Child's Pose

ting on the mat every morning.

I began with the videos and practiced with them daily, then twice a day, for a couple of months. Slowly my breathing improved, I began to relax, and my flexibility increased. When you hold a pose, you are improving your focus and strength. I had some rocky points where I felt fatigued; Ronald Yee, I found, holds his poses longer than some of the other instructors. This gives you time to attempt the pose without feeling rushed. Once you transition smoothly from pose to pose, this longer time holding the poses can be very tiring. This exhaustion limited my practice, creating a great challenge for me. Then I took another avenue in my discovery of yoga.

When I felt I needed to challenge myself more to continue the practice with enthusiasm, I used a book my wife found at the library and practiced, *Moving Towards Balance: 8 Weeks of Yoga with Rodney Yee*. It really helped me take more ownership of the practice. I read about the poses and understood more of the physiology of yoga. I redirected my focus away from the breath and refined the poses without the exhaustion I had felt while completing his videos.

Reading was another way to deepen my understanding of yoga. I completed the book in less than eight weeks because of my excitement, completing almost all of the poses with success. However, my flexibility still limited me in some of the more challenging poses. So don't worry if there are poses you are unable to practice because they are secondary to the practice. Again, just relax into child's pose or skip these difficult positions.

I felt more confident in some of the arm balances and inversions. I could hold my head stand for minutes at a time, as well as my handstand against a wall. Finally, I did an elbow stance against the wall as well. This is where you hold yourself facing the wall with only your elbows and forearms as you lift your legs, raising up and falling backwards towards the wall. I am able to pull my legs away from the wall now, but I still need the wall for my handstand. These poses are very difficult, and I would not suggest any yoga without consulting with your physician before beginning. I felt success in these poses, but you might find success in some of the poses I was unable to do because of the flexibility involved.

The Proven Power of Yoga
Cardiorespiratory function improved in subjects after only three months of yoga; and these same people scored higher on psychological profiles, which clearly correlate to an improved quality of life.

Harinath et al, 2004

Additionally, using a program keeps you grounded when your mind wants to convince you otherwise. After a few months of the videos and then his book, you are probably ready for a change. I suggest any of Baron Baptiste's videos. You can move away from holding the poses and move to a faster paced practice. He gives you a new perspective. I find his commentary very supportive, although it may make you uncomfortable at first as it did for me. He is excited about the practice and very free in his use of his yogic language. He is not burdened, as I was, in my closed-minded thinking. This is when you need to give into the practice and accept the language. It helped me to feel the inner body.

After months of working between the two instructors, I slowly began to try new videos. I did not like all of them and narrowed my instruction to three teachers I enjoy: Brian Kest, Shiva Rea, and Duncan Wong. The transitions to all these different styles of the practice were difficult, and I felt doubts with all of them. My practice is evolving, and I have given Yee's videos to other members of my family to help them begin their practice.

Now while I practice, I have one focus—self acceptance. I have resisted my desires to refine the poses with continuous effort as I have in the past. I now bring my awareness to my breath and the inner body. As I discussed in meditation, the breath is the vehicle to ending incessant thinking and the medium used to help you feel the inner body. With these two gifts, I alleviate many stresses of my life. I find myself at peace on the mat. I am less focused on improving my inversion poses and flexibility, although they are both progressing without additional effort. My devotion is all that matters, and it has allowed me to accept my current skill and conditioning.

> **The Proven Power of Yoga**
> *Participants in a study of yoga reduced their depression unlike the contrasting control group. The study also showed yoga increases flexibility as well as balance.*
> *Galantino et al, 2004*

How I Have Overcome the Traps of the Ego

There are many traps to avoid during the first year of your practice. I fell subject to many of them. As I have mentioned, I was very concerned with my appearance and focused on the poses more than I should have. My wife and I were opening our new business, the Sandlot, in Georgia. Because I wanted to make yoga practical to the average person, I wanted to ensure I had great form and forced the issue. My practice did not develop as well as it has since I stopped attempting to perfect the poses.

Previously, I did not realize that my limited skill in the poses shows how powerful the practice is. Although it is apparent I am a novice, I still receive the benefits that an expert practitioner obtains while practicing. I have accepted that all our bodies are gifts and are naturally perfect. I am able to do arm balances my wife finds difficult and she attempts the poses that require the flexibility I have yet to find. Our differences do not make one of us better than the other in yoga. Practice to practice and leave your aspirations and preconceived notions at the door. I cannot stress this enough to you as you begin the practice. Dedicate yourself to the practice alone.

Yoga is not a fad; it has been around longer than most religions. It is a timeless practice that was kept secret because of the power it has to change lives. As the plantation owners kept literacy from the slaves, many have kept these Eastern practices locked away from those they thought were unworthy Westerners. However, talking to local yoga instructors and even listening to interviews on the videos could have turned me off to this pillar had I not been devoted to the practice. My naturally cynical mind might have ended it all.

The Proven Power of Yoga
A study found that a 12-week period of yoga improved the quality of life by reducing stress in the subjects. Positive moods increased while alcohol dependence and appetite decreased. Participants felt their lives were better and wanted to continue to practice, which was the complete opposite of the control group.
Sareen et al, 2007

Some people involved with yoga can become too intense in their promotion of what they consider the answer to their problems. They seem to dramatize the practice. Being raised in Cleveland and having the closed-minded Northeastern mentality, I found the conversations of people who love yoga overly artsy; their personalities seemed a little transparent. I am not implying that they are; but from my skeptical and jaded perspective, this is how it emerged. Remember that whatever these people say or whatever reasons they may have for practicing yoga are not relevant to your personal practice.

I was going to open a wellness program to make yoga practical, as I said. I saw that many people are strong in their ways and could really benefit from yoga, but they do not seem to get over the general feeling of the yoga studio. It freaks them out because yoga does not seem to fit into our conservative thought patterns. If you find that you are one of those people, the practice at home can be the cure for you.

Working at home allows you to begin yoga with no one judging you. You will also not be overwhelmed by the culture surrounding yoga. Yoga in itself is enough. You do not need anything else. You do not need to buy the clothes, the lifestyle, or anything else; you can just practice. Some people find all these extras appealing; if you are motivated by them, so be it. However, they are all irrelevant to the importance of the actual practice.

After you have had success with Baron Baptiste, I suggest the three teachers who I enjoy so much. Brian Kest, Shiva Rea, and Duncan Wong have allowed me to open up and enjoy the practice more and more. I think I would have been overwhelmed if I had started my practice using their DVDs because they require more skill and flexibility, which I lack. Their pace is much quicker than Yee's. They also have strong personalities, which may plague you. After establishing my practice, I could see their wisdom and respect their knowledge. I love the trance dances that Shiva leads, and her way with words is almost hypnotizing.

When my wife gave me a dance-oriented video for our anniversary, I admit it really threw me off. I was originally disappointed in the gift. How ignorant I was! That video has helped my practice so much. I hate dancing more than anything; but because my wife loves it so much, I tried to learn with my wife in a swing club in Atlanta. We learned a couple of steps but did not feel comfortable during the classes. I should say I did not feel comfortable because the instructors wanted us to dance with other people. My wife was so wise to buy the videos because she knew I was now ready. It took me a while to gain enough courage to try the video, and my insecurity led me to close the blinds of my apartment. Nonetheless, the first time I attempted the video, I was hesitant.

As time goes on, I feel my inner body so much more because of the dance. I previously would not let my wife in the room if I was using the DVD because I was so embarrassed. Now I will occasionally practice with my wife. I don't worry about putting down the blinds in my apartment when I dance. I realize now how silly perception is although, just like many others, I allow it to get the best of me at times. But now I have overcome all the traps as you will too!

Yoga Brings Balance to My Life

Yoga has awakened me to the importance of practicing all the pillars. It has balanced my life. After I devoted myself to the practice, I realized that the language the instructors use allows me to open up my breathing and practice with more awareness. I thank you, Rodney, Shiva, Baron, Brian, and Duncan. I hope to continue to learn from your teachings.

I wake up every morning and practice before I do some stretching and calisthenics. The practice of yoga has increased my strength and ability to meditate with greater focus. It has also allowed me to sense my inner body more than when I began to meditate.

If I could convince you of only one pillar to try, yoga would be it. It has empowered me to open up to my creativity, improve my meditation, have the strength to continue my running practice without needing to race, improve the quality of life around me, increase my ability to learn and read with higher retention, and increase my spirituality. It is by no means a cure-all, but it is very effective in accelerating the practice of the other pillars.

Finally, yoga improves flexibility, strength, focus, conditioning, and acceptance in life both mentally and physically. Yoga is a rehabilitating process that enables great amounts of healing to take place. Previously, flexibility was something I did not respect, a gift not everyone could obtain. I was wrong. Yoga increases flexibility. Physical strength cultivated by the practice of the standing and core poses improves posture and comfort. The mental strength that is obtained is priceless.

This focus manifests in all parts of your life because yoga requires concentration in the balancing poses, which is unparalleled. These balancing poses fortify the core, which again creates better posture and overall conditioning. It empowers people to improve in other physical activities, from running to golfing. This core strength prevents back injuries that are so common in this day and age.

Additionally, there is an acceptance and an awareness of the present moment. All the great teachers explain that whatever form your body may take is perfect just the way it is as long as you keep the breath as your focus. You are perfect just the way you are; the pose is inferior to the experience itself. The practice is what is important, as is the fact that you are taking the time to be who you truly are. I have learned that my form improves without additional effort, and I accept where I am.

Where am I you may ask. I am where I need to be: on the mat daily. At times my practice suffers from forcing the poses although, as I become reborn I learn to accept my body as it is without judgment. Consequently, I have never been more comfortable with the way I look because I am not working to acquire any special outward skill. I am in the now, which brings both inner peace and contentment to my life.

Meditation allows me to control my attention and not fall victim to my ego. Running releases the stress in my life, but yoga centers my life while calming and strengthening my body. It expands my thinking and opens my understanding of the complexities of life. It allows me to realize the overall simplicity of life now that I am not distracted by the mind. There can be no drive to obtain anything from the practice or to improve anything in yourself. The goal must be the practice and acceptance alone.

I don't have any great expertise in yoga. If you saw me on the mat in the morning, you would probably be surprised. Even with all this practice, I am still unskilled in the poses; but I have gained so much more through yoga than can be written or seen. The difference between yoga and lifting and many other exercises that improve the way you look is that yoga improves the way you feel. Your body will naturally heal itself as you bring new balance into your life; you will look and feel better. You don't have to focus on your imperfections because you come to accept your body with unconditional love. Yoga balances the mind, body, and spirit.

I declare the truth and give thanks.
I am perfect as I am in this very moment.
I am beautiful, strong, unconditionally loved, and accepted.
I am _____.
And I am choosing to be happy today.

Thank you for this very breath.
Thank you for allowing me to practice.
Thank you for the abundance of wealth, relationships,
and well-being in the world.
Thank you for _____.

I close my eyes and envision
My dream.
I see myself achieving my goal to become a Renaissance *Man or Woman*
And to _____.
I visualize my newly fulfilled life.

I feel
The gift of this dream and my goal becoming a reality,
The one loving consciousness, which flows through our universe,
Full of unconditional love and acceptance
And this abundance of *(God)* energy.

Celebrate.
Smile.
Have fun
and feel the joy of living.
I give thanks for receiving all of this.
I give thanks for my greater purpose and the overall balance in my life.
And I give thanks for _____.

I declare
My purpose, established by
(*God, a higher power, or the universe*)
Is to spread unconditional love and acceptance through

_____.

I will constantly be reborn to this moment
without memory or judgment.
I will share all my wealth, relationships, and overall well-being
to improve the quality of life around me.
My (*day, evening, or* _____.) will be enjoyable and fulfilling!

Additional Suggested Resources

Glasser, William. *The Positive Addiction.* New York: Perennial Library, 1976.

This is a great book to read to understand the importance of positive addictions such as running, yoga, and meditation. It has helped me realize why I love these practices but also why at times I have stopped running, meditating, or practicing yoga. This is also where I gained the idea of how to gain strength from these practices to overcome my own weaknesses by continuing these addictions and increasing my strength exponentially.

Yee, Rodney, & Zolotow, N. *Moving Towards Balance: 8 Weeks of Yoga with Rodney Yee.* Emmaus, PA: Rodale, 2004.

This book really allowed me to take ownership of my practice. During the time of my practice in this program, my yoga flourished. I was able to move past the idea of the perfect pose and to feel the inner body as I practiced. It helped me to open up to yoga without fear or displeasure. When you are ready for a challenge or if your practice is lacking, this is a great program to drive you back on course.

Beginner DVDs

I suggest anyone who is not an active athlete start with these beginner DVDs. If you have any serious back, knee, or major deficits, A.M. Yoga for Beginners led by Rodney Yee; P.M. Yoga for Beginners led by Patricia Walden would be the least difficult DVD to begin with. Remember, if any of the poses causes you to be fatigued or you cannot continue a pose, rest. The next time you may be able to complete more of the DVD. There is no rush. You have the rest of your life to practice, so don't force anything.

Yee, Ronald, & Walden P. A.M. *Yoga for Beginners led by Rodney Yee; P.M. Yoga for Beginners led by Patricia Walden.* Santa Monica, CA: Living Arts, 1998.

Yee, Ronald. *Back Care Yoga for Beginners.* Santa Monica, CA: Living Arts, 1998.

Power Flexibility Yoga for Beginners: Stretch, Flow, Release. Santa Monica, CA: Living Arts, 1999.

Deason, S. *Yoga for Beginners: Lower Body, Abs, Upper Body.* Santa Monica, CA: Living Arts, 1999.

Intermediate DVDs
If you have previously practiced yoga before or you think you have adequate strength and flexibility, these videos are the next step in this pillar. Again, some of the previous videos mentioned can be used at all levels, and the videos to follow can be flexible in this manner as well. The key is to find teachers who make the practice feel comfortable and safe. It doesn't matter who you choose out of all these teachers. What matters is that you enjoy their teachings and are motivated by their instruction.

Batiste, Baptiste. *Power Yoga Level 1, The Initial Challenge.* New York: Good Times Home Video, 1998.

Power Yoga Level 2, The Next Challenge. Bryn Mawr, PA: Baptiste Power Yoga Institute, 2003.

Power Vinyasa Yoga/ Level 1 Beginner. New York: Good Times,2004.

Rea, Shiva. *Creative Core Abs.* Cincinnati, OH: Acacia, 2006.

Yoga Trance Dance. Cincinnati, OH: Acacia, 2006.

Wong, Duncan. *Awakening Level.* Cincinnati, OH: Acacia, 2006.

Yee, Ronald. *Yoga Conditioning For Athletes.* Broomfield, CO: Gaiam, 2001.

Yoga Burn. Broomfield, CO: Gaiam, 2005.

Advanced DVDs
Some of these videos have some beginner and intermediate practices, but I have found they are difficult to start practicing with no prior experience. I really have enjoyed the transition into these practices. Furthermore, I still am unable to complete certain poses in all of the videos listed. Do not attempt any pose you are not ready for. Give yourself time to develop. Again, there is no rush. You have the rest of your life to practice. If you saw me practice, you would understand that even with years of practice you still can be limited in the poses, but it should never hold back your practice.

Kest, Brian. *Power Yoga.* Burbank, CA: Warner Brothers, 2004.

Rea, Shiva. *Yoga Shakti.* Boulder, CO: Sounds True, 2004.

Wong, Duncan. *Source Power.* Cincinnati, OH: Acacia, 2006.

Yee, Ronald. *Advance Yoga.* Broomfield, CO: Gaiam, 2006.

Chapter 10

An Awakening and Rebirth of Your True Self

Through our study of the various perspectives of the truths of this world, you have become aware of how to obtain a full life. You are ready to be constantly reborn to this moment without memory and judgment. Through the awareness of the law of attraction and the declaration of your dreams, you are able to put all this into practice. Once you have taken the steps to empower yourself to become a Renaissance Man or Woman, you will accomplish many aspirations in life. This rebirth will take place in many forms.

Furthermore, knowing different perspectives has allowed you to incorporate not only forgiveness, acceptance, relationship, gratitude, unconditional love, awareness, purpose, affirmations, and choice but also an overall balance to anchor your life. We are one, and we should always work to improve the quality of life around us through all these perspectives and enduring understandings.

> *Nothing great was ever achieved without enthusiasm.*
> —*Ralph Waldo Emerson*

Although some truths are more alluring than others, don't be fooled into thinking that one is better than the other. They are all one in the same; their only difference is the words used to describe them.

Let's take a minute to pretend that you believe purpose is all you need in life. Just imagine you are a surgeon, which gives you the sense of purpose to help others. Then one day you are in an accident that cripples your body. You are no longer able to use your hands to improve the quality of life around you. Knowing the practices of acceptance and relationship will help reestablish your life; you won't fall victim to losing all you believe in. You can rely on gratitude for your breath in this very moment and the unconditional love your family gives you. You can make affirmations that you are still beautiful, strong, unconditionally loved, and accepted even though you have lost your gift. Additionally, you can ask what you can learn from this. With this positive attitude, you will be able to accept your new life by forgiving the one who crippled your body. This will bring you back to the present moment, and you will regain balance as well as purpose in your life through the law of attraction. You will be reborn into the now. Remember, nothing is permanent in this life. You should never put all your eggs in one basket. Use all these perspectives to motivate yourself to achieve the life you have always aspired to have.

It is essential to change your thinking and your actions in a spiritual manner. Improving one will bring limited fulfillment; but if you allow all of this to come into your life, you will obtain unlimited abundance in all areas. When I first began meditating, I had my first glimpse of this because I was also changing my inefficient thought patterns. I was able to fall in love with Ashley and spread my unconditional love. My life felt complete and whole again; I accepted my life as it was, reverencing every moment. However, I slowly lost this new awareness because of my lack of balance in maintaining my new thought patterns, positive action, and spirituality. Even though I continued to discover new pillars, as I found one, I left the previous one behind.

Every now and then go away, have a little relaxation, for when you come back to your work your judgment will be surer. Go some distance away because then the work appears smaller and more of it can be taken in at a glance and a lack of harmony and proportion is more readily seen.
—Leonardo Da Vinci

I used visualization and gratitude rarely; and although I maintained the practice of reducing my stress, my relationships were failing. I used the new pillars to exhaustion until I read Glasser's *Positive Addiction*. I realized I needed to practice all the pillars, and to not allow my mind to sabotage any of the positive habits

I had begun. The more I expanded myself into all of the different practices, the more strength I obtained.

At last, after reading Rhonda Byrne's *The Secret*, my body came alive; all was transformed. I was yet again reborn. I had found the key to all my past successes and failures. I realized that your thoughts, actions, and spirit need to be in balance. One is no greater than another. I have balanced the universal truths to improve my thought patterns, and I am avidly practicing all the pillars to bring me to a state of spiritual equilibrium. I am fulfilled, and there is an overall increase in abundance in my life, which I continuously receive and celebrate through my awareness and use of the law of attraction.

The goal of the seven pillars of strength is to keep you from being overtaken by the lie, which has led to so much destruction in the world. This egoic thinking is created by the mind, which floods our consciousness with negative thoughts and will only lead us to manifesting the lie in a new form. This is why we need to find techniques to stop this process.

This is where the seven pillars of strength come into play; they have a common goal that is to end this downward spiral. The practices are not weapons used to fight the lie that has overtaken you because this only leads us to manifest the lie in a new form. Instead, we need to put our effort into the seven pillars of strength rather than trying to solve this problem directly.

Most authors have very high expectations of their readers, as do I; but I also realize that some of us need more direct instruction concerning where to begin. The pillars are positive actions; they move you away from dwelling on the problem. Start practicing and enjoying and don't get caught up in the words you are reading, even those on this very page. Shunryu Suzuki stresses in *Zen Mind, Beginner's Mind* how the words are only a guide; the process is what really matters (2001). Never get caught up in the endless distractions. Don't judge someone's way; just find what works for you.

If you have watched Patch Adams as I instructed earlier, you may recall another great line from the movie, which always sneaks into my consciousness. In the scene before he leaves the institution to which they are both committed, Arthur

Mendelssohn, the world renowned scientist, asks Patch a simple question, "How many fingers do you see?" Finally, he explains to Patch, "You can't see the solution if you look at the problem." Patch instantly realizes that when you see in a "new light," there are many possibilities. Then he looks past the four fingers and sees eight (Williams et al 1999).

We look for a quick fix to the mundane feeling of our lives. We want an answer, a plan, a leader, a church, a government, a boss, or anything else that will change our lives. If only—if only I could pay off the credit card bills, find a better job, have taken school more seriously, have realized that this is not what I wanted—the thoughts continually flood your mind. All of them just distract you from becoming aware of all that matters: this moment, this breath. The rest is just background music.

The problems could be endless. I am sure you could talk to me for the next hour, week, month, year, or even decade about the problems; but nothing will come of this. Yes, we all have them no matter if you are black, white, man, woman, rich, poor, Christian, Muslim, young, or old. They overwhelm our days and cause us and the people around us to suffer. Cancer, bankruptcy, the church, and everything else are the reasons we think we are unhappy. Those things are only being drawn to you through your incessant thinking. We think about the major problems in our life over and over again; so the universe, through the most powerful law of them all, brings you more. Sorry but that is the reality of all this.

Therefore, forget about them; they are irrelevant. Wake up. That is all you have to do. Rise up and become a Renaissance Man or Woman. You have the choice to live your life as you want to live it. Knowing this allows you to realize that no one can stop you from accomplishing your dreams. Then you need to release them and take a break from this insanity.

Our unconscious minds react constantly to endless stimuli throughout the day. We react to our emotions, families, jobs, and anyone who we feel has maltreated us. Expectations of how life should be are the cause of these reactions. Our negative thoughts promote negative actions. Lack of awareness breeds fear and fear leads to reacting, which builds the strength of the ego. The ego needs you to react to a comment made by a friend or family member. It empowers itself to stay in control of your life. It runs rampant throughout the day, making you honk when someone cuts you off, telling you how oppressed you are, and filling your mind full of doubt.

From this moment on, we need to build the groundwork for the rebirth of your newly fulfilled life by celebrating and giving thanks for all your accomplishments. This rebirth needs to be completely empty of the ego and any past failures because they were only opportunities to learn from. So take what is needed and move on. Accept yourself as you are with unconditional love and compassion. Make a declaration this instant that you will stop listening to the voice in your head. You will no longer fall victim to incessant thoughts.

Modify your schedule by waking up earlier or spending less time watching television. Take out all the unnecessary time spent at work complaining by leaving when these conversations begin; stay out of the teachers' lounge, so to speak. Spend time you might have listened or watched the news to read and learn. Stop going to the gym and start running or walking in nature, saving the time it takes to commute to a place where most people

> *Start by doing what is necessary, Then what's possible, And suddenly you are doing the impossible*
> *—St. Francis of Assisi*

try to be whatever they feel they are not. When you are on the trail, you are not constantly comparing yourself to other people in the gym or staring in a mirror listening to the criticizing voice in your head. Turn off your cell phone and listen to a book on CD or your MP3 player during your commute home. End your evenings on the mat doing yoga or on the floor meditating, calming the mind for more comfortable sleep.

When boredom arises, pull out your pen to write or your brush to paint instead of snacking. Read a book when you can't sleep instead of continuously thinking about your problems. The more creative you are with your time, the more you will be able to practice the seven pillars of strength, and you will find you have more time than you ever felt possible.

You will be content and efficient in your life; your relationships will take precedence in your life. Smiles, tears, and laughter will find themselves flooding into your day. You will have moments of satisfaction that cannot be explained in words. The sun will be brighter because your vision will be clearer. Your life will come alive all over again. You will awaken from the dream and see the truth without effort. You will be constantly reborn without memory or judgment.

You will take control of your life because you now realize you have the choice to do so. You will choose to have a positive attitude, and you will replace negative thoughts with visualizations of the truth. You will use the seven pillars of strength to find who you truly are. You will stop paying attention to the negative thoughts, which now infest your mind, and start smiling with a sense of gratitude for all you have. Love yourself just as you are with no conditions and with complete acceptance. Take action in your life; make the choices that have to be made to accomplish your dreams.

Begin the path of the seven pillars of strength. Look past the problems. You can come up with a million reasons why you can't change your life; however, personal choice and your positive attitude make it more than possible. You are the only one who can change your life; your wife, your husband, your boss, your spiritual leader, and I are just in the shadows. You are on the front line. You have to make the choice to begin the process. It is not an easy path with your current thought patterns, but replace them with new, more efficient practices. I guarantee it is worth the effort.

Every day after that choice won't be perfect and that is okay. You have the strength to face the hard times with a laugh, a smile, and a few tears. When negativity allows imperfection to persist, your added awareness will allow the universe to bring it to an end. Live in the present and forget the past; don't worry about the future because the only moment you have control over is this one. Become a Renaissance Man!

Begin your seven-day boot camp today. You are ready for your rebirth. I suggest you begin this voyage on a Saturday or Sunday because you will have more time to read and practice as you start. Embark on rereading these chapters of this book: "How to Use This Book," "Introduction to the Renaissance Man," "The Universal Truths," and this chapter anytime during the week when you need more motivation. Reread the chapter on meditation the first day. This will give you an abundance of energy to drive the practice. Then read the following pillars each day, ending with yoga on the seventh day. Make a schedule for the boot camp, making time for the practice of all seven pillars.

Although you may practice some of the pillars already, now you will bring a new awareness and acceptance to them. I highly suggest you practice meditation and yoga daily. Running should be scheduled at least five times during the week. Improving the quality of life will be more of a daily practice, which does not have to be scheduled; but I do suggest giving at least seven written compliments in the first week. Then see if you can carry this throughout the month; this idea is from Tom Rath and Donald O. Clifton's book, which was discussed earlier. Make sure each compliment is "individualized, specific, and deserved" (2004, p.80). Reflect on your spirituality and creativity for at least half an hour each day. Then put in an hour block for the actual practice of those pillars. For example, you could plan on going to a community-oriented event for the practice of spirituality and a drama class for creativity. Time scheduled for learning should be spent rereading this book. After boot camp, follow the suggestions provided in chapter 4.

You need to allow at least one to two hours a day to begin this process, but dedicate as much time as you can. Be sure your family knows the importance of this practice in your life. You do not have to explain exactly what you will be doing, but ask for their support in any way they can offer during this time. Take a vacation from work as you begin, if possible. Pay to have a babysitter watch the kids if you have to. Wake up two hours earlier to find the time.

I will leave you with this: You are an awesome individual, and I know this because you are perfect just the way you are. Love is inside your heart, and the universal energy flows from you to me. I envision the beauty in your eyes. I find joy in knowing you will have so much fun practicing the pillars. Remember, the practice is fun and you should feel joy in every pillar because when you figure out what you enjoy, you will share this with the entire world. The universe created you to enjoy your life and to celebrate its very existence. Every breath you take is one more moment of perfection. Find yourself and share it with all who love you and even with those who appear not to do so. Your rebirth is wonderful! Feel it, be thankful for it, and ask for more. The universe is waiting for your command!

I am so overjoyed for you, and I hope to hear your story. Thanks for all you have given me and for bringing more fulfillment to my life. I love you for the wonderful person you are. Now it is time for you to begin.

I declare the truth and give thanks.
I am perfect as I am in this very moment.
I am beautiful, strong, unconditionally loved, and accepted.
I am _____.
And I am choosing to be happy today.

Thank you for this very breath.
Thank you for allowing me to practice.
Thank you for the abundance of wealth, relationships,
and well-being in the world.
Thank you for _____.

I close my eyes and envision
My dream.
I see myself achieving my goal to become a Renaissance *Man or Woman*
And to _____.
I visualize my newly fulfilled life.

I feel
The gift of this dream and my goal becoming a reality,
The one loving consciousness, which flows through our universe,
Full of unconditional love and acceptance
And this abundance of *(God)* energy.

Celebrate.
Smile.
Have fun
and feel the joy of living.
I give thanks for receiving all of this.
I give thanks for my greater purpose and the overall balance in my life.
And I give thanks for _____.

I declare
My purpose, established by
(*God, a higher power, or the universe*)
Is to spread unconditional love and acceptance through
_____.

I will constantly be reborn to this moment
without memory or judgment.
I will share all my wealth, relationships, and overall well-being
to improve the quality of life around me.
My (*day, evening, or* _____.) will be enjoyable and fulfilling!

Sources

Adamu, Bature., Sani, M., & Abdu, A. "Physical Exercise and Health: A Review." *Nigerian Journal of Medicine, 15* no. 3 (2006): 190-6.

Batt-Rawden, Kari., & Tellnes, Gunnar. "Nature-Culture-Health Activities as a Method of Rehabilitation: An Evaluation of Participants' Health, Quality of Life and Function." *International Journal of Rehabilitation Research., 28* no. 2 (2005): 175-80.

Beckwith, Michael. "The Reaction to the Secret." By Oprah Windfrey, *The Oprah Winfrey Show*, NBC, Harpo Productions, Chicago, February, 16, 2007.

Bormann, Jill., Smith, Tom., Becker, Sheryl., Pada, Laureen., Grudzinski, Ann., & Nurmi, Elizabeth. "Efficacy of Frequent Mantram Repetition on Stress, Quality of Life, and Spiritual Well-being in Veterans." *Journal of Holistic Nursing, 23* no. 4 (2005): 395-414.

Byrne, Rhonda. *The Secret.* New York: Atria Books, 2006.

Campbell, Joseph. *The Hero With a Thousand Faces.* Princeton, NJ: Princeton University Press, 1973.

Carlson, Linda., & Garland, Sheila. Impact of Mindfullness-Based Stress Reduction (MBSR) on Sleep, Mood, Stress, and Fatigue Symptoms in Cancer Outpatients."*International Journal of Behavioral Medicine, 12* no. 4 (2005): 278-285.

Csikeszentmihalyi, Mihaly. *Flow: The Psychology of Optimal Experience, Steps Towards Enhancing the Quality of Life.* New York: Harper and Row, 1990.

Damodaran, Aswath., Malathi, A., Patil, N., Shah, N., Suryavansihi, & Marathe, S. "Therapeutic Potential of Yoga Practices in Modifying Cardiovascular Risk Profile in Middle Aged Men and Women." Journal of *Association of Physicians of India, 50* no. 5 (2002): 633-40.

Diabetes Prevention Program Research Group. "Reduction in the Incidence of Type 2 Diabetes with Lifestyle Intervention or Metformin." *New England Journal of Medicine,* 346 no.6 (2002): 393-403.

Dreyer, Danny, & Dreyer, Katherine. *Chi Running: A Revolutionary Approach to Effortless, Injury-Free Running.* Fireside, NY: Simon & Schuster, 2004.

Frankl, Viktor. *Man's Search for Meaning: An Introduction to Logotherapy.* New York: Simon & Schuster, 1984.

The Will to Meaning: Foundations and Applications of Logotherapy. New York: Penguin Books, 1988.

Galantino, Mary Lou., Bzdewka, T., Eissler-Russo, J., Holbrook, M., Mogck, E., Geigle, P., & Farrar, J. "The Impact of Modified Hatha Yoga on Chronic Low Back Pain: A Pilot Study." *Alternative Therepeutic Health Medicine,10* no. 2 (2004): 56-9.

Glasser, William. *The Positive Addiction.* New York: Perennial Library, 1976.

The Quality School: Managing Students Without Coercion. New York: Harper Collins, 1998.

Choice Theory: A New Psychology of Personal Freedom. New York: Harper Collins, 1998.

Gross, Cornelius., Kreitzer, Mary Jo., Russas, Valerie., Treesak, Charoen., Frazier, Patricia., & Hertz, Matthew. Mindfulness Meditation to Reduce Symptoms After Organ Transplant: A Pilot Study."*Advances in Mind-Body Medicine, 20* no. 2 (2004): 20-29.

Harinath, Kangal., Malhotra, A., Pal, K., Prasad, R., Kumar, R., Kain, T., Rai, L. & Sawhney, R. "Effects of Hatha Yoga and Omkar Meditation on Cardiorespiratory Performance, Psychologic Profile, and Melatonin Secretion." *Journal of Alternative and Complementary Medicine,10* no. 2 (2004):2 61-8.

Hicks, Esther & Hicks, Jerry. *The Law of Attraction: The Basics of The Teachings of Abraham.* Carlsbad, CA: Hay House, 2006.

Kennedy, James., Abbot, R. Anne., & Rosenberg, Barnett. "Changes in Spirituality and Well-being in a Retreat Program for Cardiac Patients." *Alternative Therapies in Health and Medicine, 8* no. 4 (2002): 64-6, 68-70, 72-3.

Kirwan, John., Kohrt, Wendy., Wojta, D., Wiethop, B., Staten, M., Ehsani, A., Hickner, Robert., & Holloszy, J. "Effect of 7 Days of Exercise Training on Insulin Action in Non-InsulinDependent Diabetics." *Medicine & Science Sports Exercise 22* (1990): S40.

Koyamada, Shin & Cruise, Tom. "It was Karma". *The Last Samurai.* Directed by Herskovitz . Burbank, CA: Warner Brothers, 2003.

Krishnamurti, Jiddu. & Bohm, David. *The Ending of Time.* New York: Harper Collins, 1985.

Malone, Thomas. & Malone Patrick. *The Art of Intimacy.* New York: Prentice Hall, 1987.

Majumdar, Marcus., Grossman, Paul., Dietz-Waschkowski, Barbara., Kersig, Susanne. & Walach, Harold. "Does Mindfulness Meditation Contribute to Health? Outcome Evaluation of a German Sample." *Journal of Alternative & Complementary Medicine,. 8* no. 6 (2002): 719-730.

Napier, Augustus. & Whitaker, Carl. *The Family Crucible: The Intense Experience of Family Therapy.* New York: Perennial Library, 1978.

Osment, Haley Joel. "That's the idea." *Pay It Forward.* Directed by Mini Leder. Burbank, CA: Warner Brothers, 2001.

Rath, Thomas. & Clifton, Donald. *How Full Is Your Bucket? Positive Strategies of Work and Life.* New York: Gallup Press, 2004.

Reynolds, Frances., & Prior, Sarah. "The Role of Art-Making in Identity Maintenance: Case Studies of People Living with Vancer." *European Journal of Cancer Care, 15* (2006): 333–341.

Rosenthal, Robert. & Jacobson, Lenore. "Teacher Expectations for the Disadvantaged." *Scientific American,* April 1968, 19-23.

Ruiz, Miguel. *The Four Agreements: A Practical Guide to Personal Freedom.* San Rafael, CA: Amber Allen Publishing, 1997.

The Mastery of Love: A Practical Guide to the Art of Relationship. San Rafael, CA: Amber Allen Publishing, 1999.

The Voice of Knowledge: A Practical Guide to Inner Peace. San Rafael, CA: Amber Allen Publishing, 2004.

Sandel, S Suzan., Judge, James., Landry, Nora., Faria, Lynn., Ouellette, Robbie. & Majczak, Marta. "Dance and Movement Program Improves Quality-of-Life Measures in Breast Cancer Survivors." *Cancer Nursing., 28* no. 4 (2005): 301-9.

Sareen, Sandhu., Kumar, V., Gajebasia, K., & Gajebasia, N. "Yoga: A Tool for Improving the Quality of Life in Chronic Pancreatitis." World Journal Gastroenterol, 13 no. 3 (2007): 391-7.

Shapiro, Shauna., Astin, John., Bishop, Scott., & Cordova, Matthew. "Mindfulness-based Stress Reduction for Health Care Professionals: Results From a Randomized Trial." International Journal of Stress Management, 12 no. 2 (2005):164-176.

Smith, Joana., Richardson, Janet., Hoffman, Caroline., & Pilkington, Karen. "Mindfulness-Based Stress Reduction as Supportive Therapy in Cancer Care: Systematic Review." Journal of Advanced Nursing, 52 no. 3,(2005): 315–327.

Suzuki, Shunryu Zen Mind, Beginner's Mind: Informal Talks on Zen Meditation and Practice. New York: Harper Collins, 2001.

Szaflarski, Magdalena., Ritchey, Neal., Leonard , Anthony., Mrus, Joseph., Peterman, Amy., Ellison, Christopher., McCullough, Michael., & Tsevat, Joel. "Modeling the Effects of Spirituality /Religion on Patients' Perceptions of Living with HIV/AID.", *Journal of General Internal Medicine*, 21 Suppl. no. 5 (2006): S28-38.

Tolle, Eckart. *The Power of the Now: A Guide to Spiritual Enlightenment*. Novato, CA: New World, 1999.

Stillness Speaks. Novato, CA: New World, 2003.

Warren, Rick. The *Purpose Driven Life: What on Earth Am I Here For?* Grand Rapids, MI: Zondervan, 2002.

Wildman, J., Kruger, A., Schmole, M., Niemann, J., & Matthaie,. *"Increase of Circulating Beta-Endorphin-Like*

Immunoreactivty Correlates With the Change in Feeling of Pleasantness After Running." *Life Sciences, 38* no. 11 (1986): 997-1003.

Williams, Robyn. "Patch's Appeal" *Patch Adams.* Directed by Tom Shadyac. University City, CA: Universal Studios, 1999.

Williams, Robyn & Harold Gould. "Look Beyond…" *Patch Adams.* Directed by Tom Shadyac. University City, CA: Universal Studios, 1999.

Wilkinson, Bruce. *The Prayer of Jabez: Breaking Through to the Blessed Life.* Sisters, OR: Multnomah, 2000.